Gypsies at the Carnival

Joan M. Steele

authorHOUSE®

AuthorHouse™
1663 Liberty Drive
Bloomington, IN 47403
www.authorhouse.com
Phone: 1-800-839-8640

First published by AuthorHouse 8/24/2011

ISBN: 978-1-4567-4664-3 (sc)

Printed in the United States of America

Any people depicted in stock imagery provided by Thinkstock are models,
and such images are being used for illustrative purposes only.
Certain stock imagery © Thinkstock.

This book is printed on acid-free paper.

Chapter One

Mounds of dirt were piled high on both sides of the trench. The low-hanging haze held the scene in its clutches. You had to cut through the gray-white shield of damp air in order to discern the men digging below.

Three men were digging. Their shovels piling the dirt neatly on either side of the trench. A fourth man was sitting to one side of a pile of the dark brown earth, smoking. The trench was still quite shallow. The digger's shoulders and heads being plainly visible above the ground.

The alley and adjoining yards on one side were strewn with dirt covering about two lots in length. Here and there the diggers had uncovered a dog bone, a curious rock—nothing more.

A handful of people stood, watching expectantly, for something to be uncovered—waiting for anything to appear. Margarite watched as shovel full after shovel full was thrown near her feet. The two women at her right were arguing about the newspaper article.

The heavier woman nearest her elbow insisted, "The newspaper said he was buried across the street from the tavern."

"No, no you have it wrong," the other repeated, "The newspaper said the tavern was in the old hotel and that stood somewhere behind us on one of these very lots."

Margarite wondered which one was right. She had only heard

of the digging today. At school, George had said some woman had come back to town with a story about seeing a man buried alive. She was quite young when she saw it. George claimed this was the second day they had been digging. But who could believe George, he was only trying to get out of working the Algebra problems.

Margarite was torn from her thoughts by the stillness. No one was saying a thing on either side of her. Everyone had turned to the left facing the faded rotting wood fence across the alley.

Everyone had turned but the lady in black who was standing at the edge of the little group, further away than any other. She was all in black, even her umbrella was black, big like a man's umbrella.

The two men had joined the man on the far left side, and they were digging with a furor. They kept striking something solid with their shovels. A thudding sound was all that could be heard. One man stopped. He was attempting to haul something up from the ground. They took turns helping—heaving and hauling—then digging around the solid object. Soon it was revealed. Only a large tree stump. Uh! And Oh's came from the small group above the diggers. It was as though everyone was disappointed because it was not a body or at least a chest as the thudding sounds had alluded to.

Disappointment seized Margarite as well. She kept staring, waiting for the stump to uncover something or perhaps change its form. The earth smell was strong in her nostrils now. As she looked up at her feet, she realized she was almost balancing on the edge of the trench. The earth was flying, drifting across the toes of her shoes. Soon it would be in the laces—the devil to clean—as she reached down to brush them off—she looked straight into the face of the one digger. His face was thin—the skin drawn very taught across the bones.

For a few moments, Margarite had the strange sensation of being swallowed up by the earth. She was falling into the pit and the earth was falling around her shoes, covering the laces and matching the pattern of her dress.

The sun broke through the haze and rescued her, pulling her body back into its warmth and light. As she drew back turning away she realized that she was alone now—the small group having dispersed upon the disappointing stumps appearance.

She squinted up at the sun, her small eyes just slits, her face screwed up in a very unattractive mask. Stumbling across the dead grass and the weeded strips she reached the sidewalk and began to run along till she came to the corner. Watching first to one side and then the other, as she picked her way across the railroad tracks and back to the newer, wider sidewalk once more. Crossing the tracks she recognized the thin lady in black. It was Grandma Helm.

The straight yet slightly stooped back of Grandma Helm loomed before her. Still, even at her age quiet tall for a woman! She must be in her late sixties or early seventies. She walked stiffly and deliberately as if every step was planned and metted out as she moved. There wasn't a loose, relaxed, unruled or unmanaged bone in her body. Margarite liked her vision of the old lady. She envied her, her obvious strength and power. She would have liked to join her and ask her about the digging, but Grandma Helm frightened her a little.

She was very like her own grandmother—tall, thin, and strong. Margarite wished to grow-up strong—be able to take care of herself, not like her own mother. Her mother was weak, sickly, and not quite there sometimes. Grandma was more like her real mother in every way.

The sun was hiding once more. Why couldn't it make up its mind. Big drops of rain fell on her head, she pulled a sweater from her book bag and plopped it over her head. The rain and her tardiness pushing her to run.

It must be nearly four o'clock. Grandma, Mother would be worried and full of questions. Why hadn't she come straight home from school? What had she been doing? Where had she been?

Now, she must explain what she was doing and why? Margarite didn't want to explain—not just yet. She needed time to think about the scene. Had someone been buried here years ago? Margarite was fired with questions, her mind was astir—one thought came after another, not allowing the first to conclude and express itself fully. The ideas were enmassed—pressed together so that no one thought was intelligible. Her face showed the agitation. Her small eyes blinked from the deliberation. Her forehead wrinkled. Her thin, tall body was picked up once more and carried along by the spirit of excitement that overflowed onto the walk.

The rain abated, almost before it had begun. The sun's overcast blending in the longish hair and flowing into the brown of the dress. She formed a brownish sprite, struggling from its hiding place.

Margarite slowed down to a fast walk. She squinted up at the sun. It was trying to come out once more. The fever within her was subsiding. The face, once more relaxed as it gazed at the familiar houses. Only one more block. Familiarity and warmth closed in once more and she was here, outside herself.

The greenness, the feathery shadows of the tall trees and the green lawns infringing upon the sidewalk gathered her into them. The long-narrow windows arranged into two's and three's were so good to see.

The next corner, there was home. She cut across the grass, stepping carefully over the damp spots, past the huge Oak, to the long porch. As she came to the longest stretch of porch at the side, she stopped short, retraced her steps and went round to the front of the house, up to the front door. This way she could steal in and walk straight down the hall and up the stairs to her room. She wanted to think about what she had seen. How could she avoid explanations? Grandma might think she had come upstairs to read after school. Maybe, Mother would believe she had just come in earlier. What a relief—there was her alibi too.

Luck was on her side as she softly closed the door and started gently up the long, steep stairs. Grandmother's voice was barely audible from the kitchen—far back in the house.

Oh so good to be home. Reaching the top, her eyes met those beloved colored panes in the rectangular window at the top of the stairs, and this time the sun had once again shut off its light leaving the colors in a gray shadow. The shadow caught the earth once more as Margarite closed her eyes to become part of the trench scene. Did the ground hold a secret, a truth? How strange that the earth's top should be so firm and strong under feet and yet it's under parts so precarious and lax.

Chapter 2

Margarite had no longer sat down on the edge of her bed to ponder the scene when her sister came into the room. It was getting close to suppertime. She was wanted downstairs to help set the table.

Reluctantly, she followed her sister down the stairs. Dori was three years younger, nine years old, thin like Margarite. There the resemblance ended. Where Margarite had a tanning skin and dark brown hair like Grandmother, Dori was blond and pale and looked more like their mother.

Margarite stared at the small flowers on the blue background of her grandmother's dress, her eyes following the pattern to the hem, right onto the polished floor. Dragging her feet, Margarite trailed onto the great expanse of golden, shining hard-wood floor.

The heat assailed her from every side and wrapped her in. The high black wood stove on the far side gave off enough warmth for the rooms beyond. The stove and floor were in partnership. They could give the illusion of light brightness, even on a dull dreary day. They liked to play at being the sun and only just nodded to the real source of light. The three long windows facing the stove, offered the only escape from this large old Victorian kitchen. Grandmother and Mother managed to shut out the outside world and create their own private world within these walls.

Grandmother was starting to spread the tablecloth out on the large table. Grandma turned, smiled, and said, "Well, there you are, have a good read did you? We missed you. Get the silverware and the dishes out, will you." Margarite complied. Dori laid the napkins out for each place setting. Everyday meals—in the kitchen! Grandma moved to the stove helping her daughter, Linney, check the meatloaf. She took over the mashing of the potatoes and told Linney to sit down while the girls finished setting the table. Linney patted her mother's shoulder and said, "I'll just put the salad on the table first."

Margarite pulled a chair out, picking it up so as not to turn-up the big rag-rug and her Mother sat down. "How was school today," she asked her daughter? Margarite shrugged her shoulders. "Well," said her Mother, "It's only the beginning of the year. It will get more interesting. My last piano student, the little Baines boy, could talk of nothing but the Carnival. I suppose Johnny is going to be full of it tonight."

"Oh, yes!," said Dori, "Pa will take us?" "I would imagine so," answered her mother.

Grandma joined them, half laughing and remarked, "Margarite, you are so glum! What's the matter?"

"If, you must know," said Margarite, "I was wondering what they found at the digging today." "Digging!" said Grandma. "Yes, George was telling us in Algebra about some widow lady who is visiting and has stirred-up everything. She demanded they dig up the area on that short street across the railroad tracks, close to where an old tavern used to be. This lady claims, some men buried a man there—some twenty years ago." "What on earth," Grandma exclaimed, "What nonsense." "What was this woman's name?" "George didn't remember the name." "Fiddle-Faddle," said Grandma. Mother stared off into space as she did sometimes and remarked, "Your father will know all about it—after all—he's on the Town Council."

"Yes, of course," said Grandma. "Margarite, Dori—go track down and tell Johnny we're almost ready for dinner. Frank will be home any moment now."

Margarite and Dori, breathless ran into the kitchen with

Johnny straggling inside. "Off for the wash-up" ordered Grandma and off he went.

Margarite sat down beside her Grandmother against the windows. Across from her sat Dori and Johnny. Father and Mother sat at each end of the table.

Grandma said grace and the dishes were passed around.

The table took up a large portion of the space at one end of the huge kitchen. Even with the windows open now, you couldn't seem to move far enough away from the woodstove.

Grandmother began the flow of conversation as usual. "Linney and I would like to start canning some of the vegetables the end of this upcoming week. Besides, we'd like to get the vegetables out of the way so we can concentrate on the fruit. I don't suppose we're going to get East of the mountains for peaches."

"No, I think not, what with the new orders for lumber for the High School and now this new Creamery that's going in."

"Pa," shouted Johnny, "Can we go to the Carnival? Steve said their going to have all the best rides—even the Ferris Wheel. And there's this knife-throwing act. Could we go tonight? I can use my own money for the rides." Johnny would have continued breathlessly but he was interrupted by father. "I'll take you before it's over. Perhaps, tomorrow, Saturday night, we'll be able to. I have a special Town Council meeting tonight."

"Oh, gee," said Johnny throwing down his fork in the middle of his plate.

"I thought there wasn't another meeting till next month," blurted Grandma.

"This digging has caused some problems. Our fine lady has gone straight to the Governor for aid."

"The Governor!" exclaimed Grandma.

"You mean your people weren't even informed," admonished Grandmother.

"Oh, we were informed, alright," said Father. "A court order arrived early this morning ahead of the road crew. It seems our important lady was sure we wouldn't have ok'd her inquiries and carried out her request to dig up the area. So she made sure what she felt should be done, would be."

Mother interposed, "You don't think there's really anything to her story, do you?"

Father put one hand to his temple frowning, "She has so little to go on. I can't see how they would be able to find the exact location, even if her story were true."

"But if she did see it happen, then the man must still be there somewhere. "It's so exciting," breathed Margarite. "What if it really did happen?" Margarite looked at her father expecting him to understand her enthusiasm and counter with a new insight or a teasing reprive. But this time he did neither. He stared at her as though she weren't there, or he hadn't heard what she had said.

Disappointed, dejected not finding her usual ally in her corner she looked into the face of her mother at her right. For a moment, Margarite was afraid her mother was ill. Her face was as white as the knuckles on her trembling hand as she lifted her fork and then laid it back on her plate. Grandma was looking at her mother too. She reached out and clasped her mother's left hand and held it for a moment. Reassuringly, she nearly whispered, "Linney it isn't the same dear. How many stories we've heard about the older rougher West and the taverns, the saloons—only another to pester."

"Frank," Grandmother said, "Surely this will be cleared up quickly and easily. This woman probably has dreams and can tell the future."

Father smiled at this. "Well, we can't object to a relative investigating a family member's disappearance. Mrs. Durante insists she beheld this sight when she was only ten." A sigh came from my mother. Grandma started to speak, she repeated Durante slowly and clapped her hand over her mouth. I turned, Grandma, "What is it?" "Too much good food, honey" and she squeezed my hand.

"Linney," asked Pa—"One of your good desserts tonight, dear?"

Mother came back to us and said, "Yes, of course Frank, that new cake you like so much."

Chapter 3

"How could such a thing as that have happened, anyway? It isn't sensible. No one would have buried...." Paul interrupted Frank, "She claims he was buried alive!" "What an outrageous claim! How could such a thing as that have happened, even eighteen, twenty years ago in our little town? What year would that have been, 1890?" asked Frank.

"We figured according to what she told us it must have happened in 1895," intruded Willie.

"Still," Frank came back—that's only eighteen years ago—couldn't have been too much different here."

"Not so strange Frank. You weren't here when that happened, but I was. There was some talk about that time—something about some of the men in the town getting up a sort of vigilante group and taking care of some gypsy fellow who was up to no good. I was eighteen at the time. I was clerking in the feed store—my first job." added Willie.

"Oh, Willie, I know you may remember hearing all kinds of things, but they were probably just threats! I can't imagine anyone carrying that out."

"Western justice was much faster, even a few years back than today." "Yes, only eighteen years back. And the courts not nearly so established and reliable. Don't forget 'The tar and feather,' happened!" said Paul.

May had lost all patience. She had to get her two-cents in. Besides she had some questions now that this was becoming fascinating. "Why would they want to harm a gypsy? What was he up to?" "This particular young gypsy was reported to be charming, handsome, and romancing too many of the young ladies," Willie explained. "Um, I see," said May.

"I thought Gypsies were like Nomads. They never stay in one place long—always on the move."

"Yes, that's true, they don't stay long in one place unless business is good, then they linger," answered Willie.

"Business, what business would they be in?" queried, May.

"Stealing," said Paul "is usually their main business." May laughed. She brushed a stray piece of hair back into place on one side.

Frank said, "What's more important is this Gypsy Lover was Mrs. Durante's Uncle."

May stood up. "So what is our plan of action?" Frank said, "Clearly to get this business checked out as quickly as possible and send Mrs. Durante packing." Agreement at the table!

Maury said, "Before we disperse this expeditious group and close the meeting, Charlie you were going to find out exactly who this Durante woman is—her connections in town." Charlie said, "Willie and I did just that. She's the little gypsy girl the Gypsies left behind at this same time. She was adopted by the old Heller couple. They raised her. She married and moved away some seventeen or eighteen years ago."

"So, she's a Gypsy herself?"

"Looks that way," answered Charlie.

"Does she look like a Gypsy?" Asked May?"

"How do Gypsies look?" asked Frank.

"Dark skinned with raving, un-trustworthy eyes and continence," replied Paul.

"That's quite a description," said Frank.

Chapter 4

Next day was beautiful. Margarite stuck her head out the window viewing the long stretch of garden almost all the way to the Clemen's house. Margarite wondered if they could make a tent over the clothesline. She was sure if she asked Grandmother the right way, she would ok it. They just needed a few old blankets.

Margarite was planning away when she remembered her decision this fall. No more playing with the kids. She was too old. She had just turned thirteen. She couldn't keep playing the old games when everyone was younger than she.

This September, when they were playing outside, after supper, it struck her—she must stop this. It was not her place anymore. It had suddenly seemed foolish to plan the whole thing, be in charge, when she knew so well how it would turn out. At the same time, she hated to give it up. It made her feel sad.

She wanted to be grown-up, but she didn't want to let go of this wonderful play. Why couldn't things last?

Besides, she wouldn't be there for Dori and Johnny—she would worry about them. Her Mother, she knew liked her—truly—almost loved her too—when she watched out for her sister and brother. A little shiver went through her thin young frame as she thought this. Why did her mother not like her, not love her? Her Grandmother said, "This wasn't so." But Margarite knew in her heart it was. She had tried to ask her mother, once—nearly a year ago—directly—why! Her mother had looked strangely and than she had simply said, 'what nonsense Margarite. Don't ask me such things,' and turned her back to her—shutting her out, leaving her standing there, the tears in her eyes.

As she got dressed, thinking back about the digging yesterday, she knew they must continue there again today. She wanted so much to go and see if they had found anything. She knew her grandmother would be on to her if she tried to leave the yard. Grandma would know without asking where she would be going. Maybe if Julie, her best friend from the end of the block came down, Grandma would let the two of them go together—that would be the only way.

Dori was up—her bed wasn't made. She would know I would make it for her when I made mine. Dori must have already had breakfast and gone out to play. Already in the swing, I bet.

She made both beds quickly and walked slowly to the long steep stairway leading to the hall downstairs.

The stain glass-window caught her attention as it so often did. She stopped a few steps down and had a good look at the oak tree, the meadow-across the street and the sky through first one color and then the other.

The kitchen was warm and cozy. It smelled deliciously of cinnamon rolls. Grandma fixed one for her and she had it with a big glass of cold milk.

Margarite sat at the kitchen table watching her Grandmother frost the cinnamon rolls. "Grandma, do you really think they'll find a man's body in the digging?"

Grandma looked over her glasses and shook her head, she doubted it. Grandma said, "The man they were looking for had most likely hopped a freight train and disappeared in the night."

"Why should he have gone," asked Margarite? "He was probably a drifter, down on his luck, out of work, only passing through. Why should he have stayed?"

Margarite liked to talk with her Grandmother. Grandma knew so many things. She answered your questions truthfully and honestly. And if it was a question, she didn't believe you should know the answer to, she would say, "Margarite when you're old enough to know and understand, I'll tell you." But, Margarite smiled, sometimes with me she forgot my age and told me a little more. Grandma truly liked and loved her, like her father did.

Margarite began again, on another track this time. "Did you ever see this man that was buried?"

"I may have, I don't know. It's possible."

"Did you read yesterday's paper, Grandma?" "No, Margarite, I haven't gotten to it. They don't always have all the facts. The paper should be on the top of the wood pile behind the stove, bring it and read it to us."

Margarite, got up, found the paper and said, "Oh here it is in the bottom right hand corner on the front page."

She read aloud, "Mrs. Durante claims her Uncle was buried "Alive" on a Saturday night in the early fall of 1895. This took place not more than a half a block from the old hotel and bar which stood on Lincoln Street only a little distance from the main railroad tracks."

Margarite started the tirade again. "Buried alive!" Grandma exclaimed, "Margarite! Oh—I don't believe," started Grandma…! Margarite interrupted with, "But the paper says this Mrs. Durante saw them do it when she was only ten years old." "What?" asked Grandma. "Let me see that paper." And she frowned as she re-read the same information aloud. "I don't believe it!" said Grandmother.

Mother stepped into the room as Grandmother was about to continue, instead she handed the paper, folding it as she did to Margarite, motioning her to put it back on the woodpile.

Margarite, understood, this was just another one of those, your Mama is here and we don't want to trouble her with any unpleasantness or worry her with anything unnecessarily.

"Margarite," said her mother, "Why haven't you taken your braids out, brushed and combed you hair and re-braided? You know we like you to be lady-like and take care of such before you come downstairs."

Margarite, hung her head. She was sure her Mother never thought of anything else but what someone was supposed to do. She left the room, to do her hair.

Chapter 5

Supper was a little rushed. Dori and Johnny were so excited. Pa had promised after dinner had settled a bit they would all visit the Carnival. It was a family affair.

Margarite wanted so to ask her Father about the digging. Grandma was psychic, each time she tried to ask, Grandma restrained her, taking hold of her arm and asking her what Julia and her family were planning for the Carnival.

It wasn't till Mother went out to cut the rest of the cake and put the water on for coffee that Grandma herself asked, Frank, "What does Paul Harmon have to say about this digging affair?"

"She was in the sheriff's office again today. She thinks they're digging in the wrong place, wants another survey. Looks as though they will be forced to check old records and maps and dig some more. Paul thinks she doesn't know what she's talking about, but his hands are tied."

"What does she look like," asked Grandma. "Short, heavyset, dark hair, dark-skinned woman. She was raised by the Heller's." "The gypsy girl they left behind?" said Grandma. "Yes," said Father.

"Where will they dig next?" Said Grandma. "I don't know," growled Father irritably.

Excited, Margarite blurted out, "They sure didn't find

anything yesterday—only some dog bones and a tree stump. They were digging all over across two backyards. The dirt was piled high on both sides of the trench. Everyone was standing around looking as if they were going to see a skeleton." Margarite could have bit her tongue.

Grandma took hold of her arm and said, "Now, why didn't you tell us you were there?"

Her father shouted at her, "No more visits to the digging! It's like fires and dog fights—a good place to stay away from."

"That Durante woman!" Dad half swore under his breath. "She intends to bring some serious accusations against certain members of the community. This whole thing is turning into a circus or carnival in itself."

"What's all the shouting about," said Mother as she sat his cake down in front of him and went round to Grandma with hers.

"Just warming up for the carnival," laughed father.

Margarite helped Dori button up her new dress, blue, drop waist, matching sash. She tied the wide, blue taffeta ribbon in her hair, keeping the bow large, holding her long blonde hair in place, hanging down her back. Dori was so pretty! The image of her mother when she was the same age, everyone said.

Margarite's dress was gray with a wide sailor collar, a long, low red sash set in. She took her wide, red gross-grain ribbon, which almost matched the sash to her grandmother's room to put it on for her.

Margarite skipped along, half running down the hall to the back of the house to her grandmother. Grandma would surely answer the one question she had to know the answer to.

Margarite fairly cornered her Grandma as she burst into her room, ribbon in hand. She nearly dropped the ribbon when she looked straight into her Grandma's eyes. There was such sadness there, and what else? "Fear," thought Margarite.

"Grandma, what's wrong?" whispered Margarite. "You look old tonight. You never look old like other grandmas."

Grandma took her face in her hands and her whole expression changed, as though she, Margarite, was an anodyne for the

15

sadness. She said, "And, well, I am old." And they both laughed and hugged.

"Let's do the ribbon," said Grandma. "I believe, Margarite, this is your first grown-up dress. We'll do something different with the hair." Grandma took the two long braids, loosened and brushed through them. Deftly, she pulled her long hair high up at the crown and braided it into one braid, turning it under, pinning it securely at the nap of her neck. Then she pulled the bowtie through at the top of the braid making a large flattish ribbon. "Now, look in the mirror. See, you look older. You are beautiful in your own special way!" "I am?" asked Margarite, astonished. "You are!"

"Why, why did they bury that man? They did bury him, didn't they Grandma?"

"Yes, Margarite, I believe they must have." "What did he do that made them bury him?" Facing the mirror Margarite imaged her Grandmother, but for the eyes. Grandmother's eyes were dark brown, snapping. Margarites were small and very green.

Turning, facing Grandmother, Grandma said, "Margarite, the reason they didn't like him was because he liked all the young ladies too much—one or two in particular, I recall! And the young ladies liked him. He was very dark and handsome. Well, perhaps not so handsome, but tall, dark and charming. He had a very appealing way about him."

Margarite persisted, "The father's didn't want their daughters marrying him?" "No, exactly, they wouldn't have allowed it. And they were right in this. He was a bad person." "How do you know this, Grandma?" "Believe me, Margarite, I just do. If any deserved to die, he was one! Don't feel sorry that he was buried. He deserved to be buried."

"Margarite," yelled Dori as she came down the long steps into the front hall landing, "You look so much older with your hair up, my! Doesn't she look older, Mama?" "Yes, I'd say older and very smart." "It becomes her, Linney, her hair up," grinned Grandma. "Yes," Linney stared strangely at her eldest daughter as she joined them.

Margarite was smiling, grinning, almost mischievously,

confidently, not shyly as was her usual smile. Linney searched the face, the eyes. She clapped her hand over her mouth to stifle the cry that built in her throat.

"What is it, Linney?," pleaded Grandma. "For a moment, I was in another time, place." She attempted to shrug it off, "seeing your daughter almost a young lady," is a shock for any mother.

"An arm for both my ladies," said father. Grandma took Dori's hand and Johnny ran along at his own pace. "Only two blocks down, and three over," instructed Frank.

Over a block away, the noise assailed them. "The tin-panny music," laughed Grandma.

The bright lights, in the beginning of twilight, the wild mixtures of bright colors, the lights of the Ferris Wheel against the night sky pulled them into this make-believe world of thrills, fantasy, and the joys of impulsive amusements. Escape from the familiar, the ordinary of their everyday world! Here for a few hours they could lose themselves, be made over, become a different person for an evening. Enchantment with just a touch of danger to tingle the fingertips, make the faces dance!

Pa bought the tickets at the front booth while each pair of eyes focused in on what hoped to be their special delight. Pa gave them each their own admission ticket. The fellow in the cage tells me there are two new rides: The swings over there, and a train car that goes all around the ballpark. There's a big clown show in the tent at the center. I think we should all go and see it first. Our admission tickets take care of it. They sat on campstools for the big show. Mother and Grandma sat down together. Mr. and Mrs. Powell turned around catching Grandma in conversation, their twin boys, too noisy as usual.

Clown crazies, acrobats, juggling, a dog act with clown hats. "Always, the same," remarked Mother. Pa laughed, "But wait, they'll advertise all the main attractions. We can see what is out there, before we trot all over to find it."

Sure enough, Johnny's 'Knife Act,' was first to show. Pa promised to go with him. Grandmother and Mother were for the beading and doll display. When Margarite and Dori saw the fortune telling sign waving, they were set to go.

Walking out, Pa spotted his foreman and family, Grandma was lost talking to her friends from her church-quilting group, while Dori, Johnny and Margarite spied the Merry-Go-Round right in front of them. The Merry-Go-Round—a had to be, first. Johnny was on his favorite horse pick before Dori could find one low enough down for her to climb on. Margarite gave her a help up and managed to breast her own, right beside Dori's on the inside. Grandma, Mother and Father sat down on one of the in-between high back seat affairs and off they spun. Two rides later and all three, smushed together on the Ferris wheel—Margarite in the center, they screamed excitedly as they went up and over. Johnny and Dori had to try the swings. Pa laughed as they disembarked a little wobbly. "Not so good on my stomach," grinned Johnny. "No seconds, thirds?" asked Pa.

Johnny had to do the train car ride around the park. Pa volunteered to go along with him. Pa cautioned, "We will all meet back on the admissions side of the big tent—no later than a half hour from now." Pa pointed out the paths to their separate delights and handed them money for tickets and a little more besides.

Dori and Margarite, hand-in-hand took their preferred path to the Fortune Tellers, giggling as girls are apt to do.

Chapter 6

The Fortune Teller's tent was way on the other side of the park. Dusk was on its way, bringing a fresh breeze and a softness to the colors, the lights. Dori was especially enchanted with the Japanese lanterns they had strung atop of two of the big displays. They had to watch the two men throwing balls at the imitation moving ducks in back of the booth. Dori had to see the prizes: Dolls, and toys—nothing new. And the lantern booth on the right had cotton candy, red, of course—they had to try it.

Reaching the Fortune Teller's Tent gave them a start—right in the center of the dark red curtains was a likeness exactly like the big printed sign of the clown's advertisement. The Fortune Teller's face full on them, powerful dark eyes, her hand beckoning them to come in. Long strands of bright beads, Gypsies dress and dark skin. "She must truly be a gypsy," remarked Margarite. Would you like to step inside and see—the head thrust out at them spoke, you can come along together? Margarite, Dori, surprised, a little startled looked into the face, very much like the picture excepting this one wore a mustache. They handed him a sticky ticket each and followed him into the tent.

They stood inside what proved to be a small entryway. Only a campstool and the paper filled this narrow space. The curtains in front of them were a sort-of-tangle of thin wispy like under curtains in a bedroom. The breeze blew them slightly billowing them somewhat at the bottom. Margarite picked out red, green, orange, yellow and purple. What a fun tent this would be to play in—you could do a play for your friends. They could sit on the ground. Their tent hadn't come off today. Grandma had promised next Saturday.

Our gypsy man held the curtains back on one side for them to enter in. He was laughing all over his face without smiling at all. How did he do this thought Margarite?

The face from the big sign loomed before them. Real, up close, the lines, the markings, what looked to be the harshness of the sun, the wind—all the harshness of the outdoors set in the tan, thin, leather of this mask. Margarite gave a little shiver. Such gaudy attire thought Margarite. Mother, Grandmother would say it could only be for the stage. The green, green of the blouse, a color Margarite loved made the skin even more repulsive. The many-colored pattern of the long skirt and dark black vest looked none too clean to Margarite. Grandma would say she needed a good rubbing down with soap and water.

This grotesque caricature motioned for them to be seated, on the faded old flower print of the strange short, backed little chairs. She, herself, settled on a similar chair across from them at the small low-down table. A peculiar shaped table—it seemed to have an extra side or two. She threw a shawl like piece, tasseled at the bottom over it and the dust flew about. Dori coughed.

Fascinated they watched her place the small crystal ball they had anticipated, on the table. Next, she took from the floor behind her an over large dark picture set of cards.

"And how shall we tell your fortune my young ladies?" Dori said excitedly, "Oh—I want to look into the crystal ball." The face smiled like the male partner without parting the lips. "For you my dear?" She turned to Margarite. "The crystal, the taro cards—she pointed to the deck, or the palm and she turned her own leathered hand palm-up upon the table." Margarite, set puzzled not answering.

"You've never had your fortune told before?" "No, no we haven't," answered Margarite. "Would you like to satisfy your curiosity and do a bit of each?" "Oh yes," said Dori, "Wouldn't we Margarite?" Margarite smiled at her little sister. "Yes, I think that would be fun," she said.

"No, no, fortune telling's not for fun answered the mask, "Fortune-telling is very serious." "Is it?" said Margarite.

The Gypsy mask didn't answer, instead, she moved her body closer, staring into the faces of first Margarite and then Dori—and again once more—scrutinizing them, boring into them with her dark, hard eyes.

"You are sisters, are you not?" "We are," they said together. "But you have strange eyes for your darker skin, they are green. Your sister's eyes are blue and her skin is very pale." Dori laughed, "My grandmother has darker skin, but she has brown eyes." "So where do you get your green eyes—your mother, your father?" "No," said Margarite, "No one knows for sure where I get my green eyes."

"Let us see what the spirit powers tell us about these green eyes of yours." Margarite smiled, Dori reached for her sister's hand and squeezed it, "Oh how exciting, Margarite." They giggled.

"My ladies, the crystal first. The crystal shows you in a corner house. A white gingerbread house with a long sunning porch. It has a marvelous colored window at the top of the stairs. I see your mother, she looks much like you and she pointed to Dori. She is very sad sometimes, but your Grandmother with the dark snappy eyes and sharp tongue protects her." They bumped heads fascinated at the reality of what she was telling them, searching within the ball to find their Mother there. Dori said incredulously—"But how do you know? I don't see my mother in the ball. I don't see anything in it." "No, you don't see her, but I have special powers. I see her." Before she thought, Margarite, said defiantly, "That is ridiculous, you know of my mother some other way, but not from looking in this glass ball. You don't have special powers. It's only a trick, like magic." "Oh," said the mask, "You have a tongue like your Grandmother's. You don't believe in special powers."

She grabbed Margarite's left hand, holding it firmly, turning it slightly so as to see from the wrist and up. The leather hand was strong, Margarite could barely move her wrist in the grip.

A strange fear like she had never known before embraced her. She was frightened to look up into this monstrous face for a moment. Dori said, "Let go my sister's hand." The mask said, "Are you frightened ladies? I mean you no harm. I hold your sister's hand only so I can read her palm. You agreed to the three in one session." Dori looked into Margarite's eyes as she looked up once more, their fright mirroring in each other's gaze.

The Gypsy woman continued, "You have a long lifeline—see how it runs," and she traced it with her bony index finger from the top most point in the palm down below the ending of the pad in the palm. Margarite recoiled, shivering at the touch. The star of Jupiter beneath the index finger, on the 'Mount of Jupiter'! Oh, yes, and the strong headline. Small, long fingered hand, fingers not so long, but still long, in comparison to the palm—do you see?"

Margarite wanted to scream, but she caught it in her throat. "Very like another hand of the green eyes, larger longer thin fingers, the eyes larger, but the same slight slant to the eyes and the wide, long slit of the mouth. Yes—your green eyes come from your father."

Margarite couldn't find words. She was caught in a spell. She heard the words, but they made no sense. Dori yelled now in fright, "Our father has blue eyes!" "Does he," said the Gypsy.

"Yvonne, did you call my name?" The dark face from the entrance appeared behind them as though from nowhere. They heard no footfall. He held up a large clump of Dori's hair—"such pretty golden hair." Dori screamed, reaching back, "Let go my hair."

Margarite swung out with her free right hand across her left, knocking the crystal ball to the ground, she screamed at her sister, "Run Dori, run back the way we came as fast as you can." Dori sprang to her feet surprising the gypsy pair, carrying out her big sister's command. Through the tent and fast as she could go she went screaming into the evening past the Japanese lanterns displayed on either side, gaining momentum as she ran.

Chapter 7

"Let go my hand, you "Old Witch," Margarite yelled and hit Yvonne a chop on the arm that held her hand. This gave her arm, her hand release, but earned her a hard slap across the face. Stunned, Margarite found her arms held behind her back before she could fully recover from the blow. She was standing now. As Yvonne lunged for her, another blow ready, Margarite kicked out hitting Yvonne a good one in the shins.

"Temple, Yvonne screamed in pain, tie her up before we have any of the late crowd. We'll close early." "All of our stuff," asked Temple? "Got to be!" In less than five minutes they were carrying their own in hand, making for their old cart and horse, tied against the tree. Margarite was covered with the inner curtains she had admired and carried in the fireman's lift on Temple's shoulder. Yvonne had the three stool chairs tied together and slung over her back, her bag of tricks in her other hand. The tent was the Carnivals.

They took the back route out, moving slowly at a jog, down to the further end of town and across the railroad tracks.

Margarite found herself tossed in the back of the van like cart, trussed up like turkey, her arms and legs tied together in back of her with heavy string. They had uncovered her face so she could breath. A dirty rag was tied over her mouth to keep her from screaming out. How could this have happened to her?

It was so fast; she was not sure how it did happen. Dori got away. She would be safe. What would Pa do? How would they find her? Would they find her? They would, like the stories she had heard of a long time ago—bring her home. She tried to move her arms and legs, but it was no use. If she hadn't been so angry, she would have cried. Oh, Grama, Margarite spoke aloud in a low voice, what will I do? What can I do?

Dori stumbled into her Pa and Johnny near the Ferris Wheel. She was hysterical, half sobbing, half screaming when she saw Pa.

"Dori, girl, what is it? Where is Margarite?" "They, they have Margarite. She can't get away."

"What on earth are you talking about Dori, talk sense? Where is Margarite?"

"At the Gypsy tent—the Fortune Tellers. She told me to run, to get away. That awful gypsy lady is holding Margarite by her wrist. She was reading her palm."

"This doesn't make sense!" Said Pa. "You just left her?" "Yes, I ran as fast as I could like she told me to do. We were both so afraid!"

"Dori," said Pa, "It will be alright. I'll go and get your sister. You and Johnny go right over there and around to the other side of the big tent where your Mother and Grandmother will be or wait a few minutes till they get there. Then stay right there till I get Margarite. I'll meet you all there. Johnny take hold of Dori's hand and stay right with her—hear me?"

"Yes, Papa," said Johnny.

Pa half ran to the Fortune Telling tent. "My Lord," he said half-under his breath, "What else might happen in the last couple of days?"

Out of breath, he stopped for a moment staring at the sign on the tent. The same as the big advertisement they had all seen. The face was fearsome.

He opened the tent, not quite believing his eyes. It was empty, except for one campstool and a flung newspaper to one side of it. The grass was flattened, dug into in spots as though there had been a fight of some sort. "It's not possible," Frank muttered. It's something out of a story. I'll go outside, and find she's there close-by, but he did not believe his own reassurance. He looked at the lantern stands on both sides not far away, only a few men—and a little boy at one and the Cotton Candy man was cleaning up in process of closing.

Frank ran to him first. "Have you seen a girl of thirteen, her hair done up, in a gray dress?" "No, can't say I have." His wife said, "Dark hair with a little blond headed girl in a pretty blue dress?" "Yes," said Frank, "My daughters, you saw them? The tallest, my oldest didn't come back with her little sister. Did you see the littlest girl come by in the last ten minutes or so?" "Well, it was busy about then, but I did look up and see a child flying by, screaming. Didn't think anything of it—children do that when they're playing."

Frank said, "Did you see the Fortune Teller leave—about the same time?"

"Yes," said the man, "They left early the last two evenings. This last hour—not much business." "Was there a girl with them?" "Nope, they were alone carrying their decorations and equipment."

"Well, then she's got to be here somewhere." He walked quickly down a ways to the next stand and asked the same questions. No one had seen anything. They had heard a child screaming—nothing strange in that.

He asked the counterman here where he would find the man in charge of the Carnival. He was told he would be at the front ticket counter tallying up.

Pa couldn't move fast enough. He found his family huddled together in disbelief, Dori crying softly. He cautioned them to stay where they were while he checked with the Carnival Manager.

Pa was near screaming himself before he made himself understood by the Manager. They sent the young boy at the ticket cage to fetch a policeman. The Manager kept saying "My God, man! It can't be a kidnapping. Things like that don't happen anymore!" He told the fellow who was picking up trash to run down and see if the gypsy's cart was still there. "Did you see a cart down a ways—from their tent—under one of those big maples?" "No, I did not," said Pa, "But of course I wasn't looking for such."

The family, all but Pa, were taken home in the Police wagon. Pa went with the Policeman back to the station. He called Paul, the sheriff. They all decided to look for the Gypsy's cart in the three main directions out of town. Pa went with Paul.

An hour and a half later they returned having found no signs of the cart, though in the darkness now this would have proved much more difficult. As Paul said, "Gypsy's were experts at covering their tracks and knowing all the obscure off-beat hiding spots in any vicinity." They'd form groups in the early morning and find them. They couldn't have gotten too far. Horseback would work best, they could cover the wooded and country areas as well as the offshoot logging roads in the larger area.

Pa went home. It was twelve o'clock. No one in bed, not even Johnny. Coming into the kitchen he could see the hope in Linney and Grandmother's eyes. He sat down at the table and Grandmother put a cup of coffee in front of him. No one spoke. They were afraid to know.

"Frank," said Grandmother finally, "No news?" "No" he said quietly. "We haven't found them. The dark was against us tonight. We will start early tomorrow and search the area all around."

"They can't have just disappeared," said Linney.

"We've prayed," said Grandmother. "The best thing now is to go to bed and get our rest so we can find them in the morning." "Yes," said Pa, "What else can we do?"

"They'll travel at night," said Linney, "While we're sleeping." "Now, Linney," said Grandmother, "You don't know that for sure."

Chapter 8

Margarite woke to the feeling of the up and down, back and forth of the cart. She felt sore all over. It felt damp and chilly. Signs of morning. She tried to kick off what she was swaddled in and realized that her hands, her ankles were not tied. The rag was off her mouth. Were they being kind? She thought not. They must have traveled a ways, that's why they had cut her bounds. They were certain she would not run away now—how could she? There was only one way out and that was locked. She knew for she had pushed herself to the slit of light, that had to be a door, kicked against it.

Yes, it must be daylight—from the cracks around the door—there was more light. She could see a little of her prison. Straw on the floor, blankets tossed in two corners, and a kind of cupboard on one side up-high, and hooks along both walls with clothes hanging—more, bright, bright colors and hideous dark prints. It smelled musty and of stale sweat, nearly as bad as a barn. Margarite shivered. What was that funny little square at the top of the door? She attempted to stand and fell back. The second time she made it. Leaning on the wall with her left hand she walked to the door. It was locked on the outside as she thought it had to be. She reached up and pushed at the square. Ah, real air, clean and keen to the nostrils. They were riding down a narrow country lane—a grass strip in the center—trees on both sides.

She didn't recognize anything familiar. On the left she found a metal brace that when you pushed up, in the center, straightened out and held the window cover out.

She sat down quickly. They had pulled off the path-road. She heard their voices now, loud. Would they let her out?

"You found the window." Temple pulled the steps down from under the wagon and threw what looked to be a heavy old braided drape pull over her head and pulled it through the loop and helped her step down.

Margarite's eyes squinted at the light. She had to admit they had chosen a pretty spot to stop. Against the rock not far away was a lovely trickling stream of water—must be from a spring. She walked toward it. Her captor allowing her to walk to the water. She reached out both her hands and let the water trickle over them. The water stung when it hit the abrasions on her wrist—little streaks of dried blood! When she thought they were cleansed she cupped her hands and threw it at her face, shaking her head to flick the droplets away. She cupped her hands once more and took a big gulp of water. How good it tasted—cold, fresh. It gave you a real flavor as it slid past the tongue. No flat tasting, cloudy liquid, this—clear and clean! Good water like Grandma always said, not like some places. She took a few more swallows. For a moment in the joy of the outside air and the drink, she forgot her predicament, her captors. Turning, she saw her drape pull was attached to a tree a few yards behind her. Yvonne was bent over a small fire in the center of an old log. Surprisingly, the smell wafting to her nostrils made her mouth water. Margarite caught another smell from behind her. Temple was painting the dark, fading red of the wagon to a sort of forest green—a dingy green as though it had been mixed with colors. Her next need brought her only one solution, she would have to walk into the trees directly in front of her.

Walking as quickly as she could she heard Yvonne's high laughter as she turned her head, the laughter brought her strength back, as soon as she had relieved herself she thought of lifting the loop over her head and running through the trees in the same direction, but as she tried to pull the cord upward, it would not loosen. She looked down at the cord and realized it was some sort of special knot. Reddening from frustration and embarrassment, she walked back.

Yvonne was throwing pieces deftly from the pan to the three plates setting on the flattish rock. Margarite couldn't believe how she was able to do this without utensils. She wondered if they would be eating with their hands. She needn't have wondered for in the next second Yvonne was pouring hot water from the kettle like device over three forks. She grinned up at Margarite. "They are as clean as I can manage." "I see," said Margarite.

"What kind of a knot is this?" asked Margarite—pulling the cord out as far as she could. "It has a name," said Yvonne. "What's important, it works!", she laughed. "You've found out?" Margarite stuck out her tongue and Yvonne laughed louder.

"Temple" she yelled. He called, "A few more minutes, go ahead."

Yvonne handed Margarite an old scarred piece of china with a burned edge, but the ham strips and the flattish cakes, like pancakes, with their own honey inside were delicious. She ate hungrily.

Yvonne turned her back for a moment, and Margarite smelled the aroma of coffee.

She squatted back down on the grass, the other side of the fire from Margarite.

Temple joined them after splashing his hands under the water of the spring. He picked up the third plate from close to the fire and sat down facing the log—viewing his paint job. "It did need a coat of paint!" And the laughter trickled in his throat as he swallowed.

Yvonne set an old tin cup of coffee on the ground near to Temple.

She took another tin cup, splashed a little hot coffee in it, rinsing it, and pouring the liquid out along the rim of the cup. She poured some coffee and handed it to Margarite, "This is what we have to drink. Our children drink coffee young. You will like it." Margarite took the coffee. She didn't dare show she was pleased for she had pestered her own grandmother to drink coffee many times before and had never gotten more than a sip. She sipped it slowly, hot and strong, stronger than grandmother's. She did like it very much. Yvonne, watching her, smiled her all over the face, not opening the mouth smile.

"Where are we going," asked Margarite. "Not too very long and you will know more about where we are going for you will be there. There's little chance you would have been there before. You will not like it. It is nothing like your gingerbread house."

"Why do you call it gingerbread," asked Margarite? "All the fuss and bother and extra decoration around the edges of the roof and around the doors and windows." "How do you know the house you said you saw in the crystal ball is ours?" asked Margarite.

"I just do," answered Yvonne. "Isn't that the way all good mother's and grandmothers answer?" The anger swelled up in Margarite once again. "You knew we would come to the Carnival all along," said Margarite. "You waited for us to visit you. You intended to steal Dori as well as me, didn't you?" Temple smiled, "The good mind of her father!"

"Settle down," said Yvonne. "Don't fight, what you can't do anything about."

This only angered Margarite more, "He's not my father! How could he be my father? Why, why do you want me? Why did you want Dori? Did you send that awful Durante woman to our town to cause trouble and dig up the ground?"

"I tell you," I'm your Grandmother," said Yvonne.

Margarite threw her coffee across the grass.

"Time to get started again," said Yvonne.

Chapter 9

Paul picked Pa up at five the next morning. Grandma handed them hot coffee in some old jars and plenty of warmed cinnamon rolls.

Paul had much to relate. Seems the major business people in town had trekked into the station all day yesterday reporting their stolen goods—two of Sam Snyder's best horses: Show the County fair winner and his pride and joy, another older horse and the little pony the Jones kid had just received, feed for the animals, and all kinds of food items—canned and otherwise, and May was screaming at the loss of some of her best cottons, and some expensive linen and silk velvet material.

"That wasn't just the one cart?" asked Frank. "Oh, no," answered Paul. "There have been three others spotted the last couple of days. They never brought their carts into town—too smart for that."

"And Frank, there's something else I have to tell you that makes matters worse." They walked back to the barn, climbed onto their horses. Sam had lent them two of his better riders. He and the rest of the group, met up at the edge of town—back exit and divided into three groups. They were all to search the least traveled routes in the surrounding area of the town, meet back here early afternoon.

"Sunday" said Frank, "What a day to be looking for your child."

"We just got word this morning from Seth in the next county, that puts a whole different outlook on this whole situation. He says they were scavenged bad in three towns about six-months ago. The Gypsies have been given an old farm spot and grounds by some old lady who befriended them two or three years ago. "Where," demanded Frank? "In Canada, right over the border. Seth and our Walt took Walt's new Ford; they're driving up there to check it out. They'll have to find the camp on foot after they get up there cause the area is all wilderness. They probably won't be allowed to go onto the grounds."

"No jurisdiction?" said Frank. "No, not just that—the Gypsies have the deed to the property, so they do not have to allow trespassers of any kind. And anyhow, a warrant would only bring denial and complete non-cooperation." "Well, that's a fine state of affairs," Frank said. "Ya, it sure is," said Paul. Walt and Seth will probably be able to see Margarite, spot her from a distance if they're up there, but that's about it."

"Do you think there's any hope at all they might not have reached there" asked Frank? "Not much," said Paul.

"The wagon, Margarite was taken in, the Carnival folks said was a faded dark red." "Yes we know, but the Gypsies have a habit of repainting, especially in circumstances of this kind. Or they could have stopped outside of town and put her in another wagon."

"My God, what a nightmare," said Frank, "How will we ever find her, get to her, bring her home."

Paul said, "Now, remember, we've got smarts too."

They were beginning to climb somewhat, the other two fellows a little ahead. After the second hour, their group found a clearing with wagon wheel marks and a spring. Two sets of wagon wheels appeared to have made this same stopover. This gave hope to their chase and they spread out and moved a little faster back and forth into the wooded areas and back onto the country road. Near ten o'clock they came into view of another group. They had spotted two stopping off spots, with the tracks of what they thought could be three different wagons, some remains of food and a fire—nothing more.

Cecil told of another little girl disappearing this way a score of years ago—never finding her again. Paul interrupted him and said, "We're faster and we don't quit looking like they used to."

Before they separated to search the known hiding spots, Sam asked Frank if there would be any reason for taking Margarite in particular. "What possible reason could there be?" answered Frank irritated at the question. "Oh, just asking," said Sam. "You know the old rumors about that Gypsy Casanova character that all the young ladies took a shine too." Frank said, "Ridiculous, because Margarite has darker skin like her Grandmother. So does Johnny for that matter. Linney was jilted by some no account fellow who took off after promising to marry her, but that would have nothing to do with this."

"The person we need to question some more is that Durante woman, maybe she's connected to the kidnapping."

Frank was all for going on up to the Divide and finding their hold-up, but Paul calmed him down. "It would take at least four, maybe five more hours. The horses will be worn out and you don't know exactly where to look. Seth does. He knows the terrain, wilderness and the old ranch. He'll be able to find out if Margarite is there, if it is at all possible. It won't help Frank. You'll be exhausted getting home in the dark and not able to function the next day. Seth said he'd call the nearest ranger station and they should relay to his office or ours."

Frank had to admit, Paul was right. He wasn't a great rider and certainly no tracker.

Coming back they found a piece of red gross-grain ribbon like the trim on Margarite's dress that had caught on a low branch, otherwise nothing of any help at the moment.

Coming together an hour later than anticipated they showed little more for their trek into the countryside. The four Gypsy wagons had disappeared, their loot in haul.

More questions, "Why did they want Margarite?" Frank answered, "Margarite saved Dori with her quick thinking. They would have taken her too."

Monday they would confront that Durante woman and find out what she knew. What she was hiding. Frank went back to the Police Station with Paul to wait for word from Seth. He'd call home and let the family know what was going on the best he could.

Chapter 10

Margarite couldn't believe her eyes when she was allowed to step down out of that smelly old box and touch the earth. It was beautiful. They were in a deep wood. It had been hours. It must be late afternoon. A little chilly, the breeze, but the air, it felt so good, so clean.

Yvonne walked ahead, while Temple led her by the drapery cord. They walked downward. She realized this nearly stumbling. She brought her eyes down to the ground where she could watch where she was going. A path opened up at her feet. The rich dark soil of the path held clutches of moss here and there as they walked in a downward direction.

Ahead an even steeper decline was bringing them into a small, but beautiful cleared, valley area. At the far side she saw an old dark brown farmhouse with a roofed porch stretching across the entire front area, like their own home, but this one only in the front. No gingerbread, thought Margarite, but still looks like home. Smoke was coming from the chimney.

Yvonne walking fast was shouting to someone in the house. A boy about Johnny's age came out and threw himself into Yvonne's arms, laughing. She picked him up in a big hug. Looking on either side, stretched out from the house and nearly part of the wood, there were old heavy weather beaten camp tents. It was a small town, the farmhouse, the main building. She saw a barn now and she thought an old milk house.

Laughter came from what must be the back of the house. On all sides they were surrounded by woods, a deep evergreen forest, with a maple, an oak, a few fruit trees on the grounds. Puppies played in a circle around a dark haired little girl of about four. It was a welter of life.

It was a shock after Margarite's strange fretful ride.

Temple had pushed and pulled her up the steps and into the old house where Yvonne was talking in another language to an old woman who looked even worse than herself, who was missing teeth and cackled with laughter as Yvonne described loudly throwing her hands every which way. Margarite determined they must be speaking French. The old lady grabbed the drapery rope from Temple and pulled Margarite around every which-way viewing her like she were a dog or a cat. Then she pulled her close and grabbed her chin roughly in one hand and shook her head repeatedly.

Before she thought, Margarite spit in her face and once again her impulsive action was returned with a hard slap that stung and made her ear ring.

Margarite found herself in Temple's charge once again and was tied to the large apple tree in back where the children were shouting and playing. They proceeded to prod and poke at her with sticks and lift her dress up and laugh.

She tried turning away from them and as she did the drapery rope grew tighter, but she managed to see the barn and a pasture behind it lying even further down, horses and a pony. It couldn't be, but it surely looked like Show, Sam's beautiful rich-brown horse, the one he was so proud of.

The children grew tired of her and let her be. They went back to their games and if it hadn't been for the good air and the beautiful scene she would have cried and sobbed for her grandma. She was so very tired and thirsty. Margarite wanted to close her eyes and pretend she was home and all was the same.

She must have fallen asleep standing. For a breeze was

touching her that made her shiver. It must be later than she had thought for the sun was fading.

The little boy, who looked to be Johnny's age or younger brought her a big bowl and sat it down on the ground. It smelled so good—looked like a stew. "Goulash," he said. He helped pull the drapery rope around, loosen it so she could sit down on the ground and eat. There was a spoon in the bowl. She asked him for water and he grinned. He took a cracked cup from a crevice on the old pump stand, rinsed it and pumped it full of water, spilling some as he brought it to her. He was an odd little fellow with so many changes in his face. He was thin and the skin on his face was pulled tight—it made him look older. He wore a sort of perpetual smile. The food, her water—to Margarite—at this point, represented an incredible kindness.

It was quite delicious. Grandma, Mother, should have the recipe. She gulped the water down. He stood a ways away and without asking, took her cup and refilled it.

She asked him his name. He grinned broadly and said, "They call me, Remos." "I'm Margarite," she held out her hand and he took it! Their skin was nearly a match.

Before she could ask him more about where this place was, Yvonne stepped out, down the steps and came to her. "Lisa will come and bring you a change of clothes and show you where you can wash—you'll like the washing-up, I'm sure."

Infuriated again, Margarite spit out, "Where are we? We must be nearly to Canada?" Yvonne laughed heartily at this and answered, "You are Louis's daughter." "Louis, my foot," screamed Margarite, "I'm Frank Cutter's daughter." "Are you," said Yvonne, "We shall see."

Lisa, a dark, dark haired girl with darker, blacker eyes than Yvonne who looked to be fourteen, fifteen maybe, untied her rope from the tree and led her away down past the pasture area and back a little ways into the trees where she heard the sound of a small creek. She laughingly took off the rope in one swift twist, helped her take off her dress. She handed her some clean rags, some clothing and a bar of soap. You can take care of yourself behind the big log jutting out into the water. Don't try to run when you're dressed you'd only run into old Limpy, our local brown bear who would scare you half to death. I'll wait for you right here. Margarite reached for her dress, but Lisa said, "No, you put on the one I gave you, It's old, but it's clean."

Margarite felt as though she were a very small child, forced to do exactly as it was told. Perhaps she was—here!

She took care of herself as best she could. She was glad that her hair was up, though strands were starting to fall from each side, it enabled her to wash her face and body parts as best she could in the shivering cold water. She was surprised the rags smelled clean. The dress was a tired old piece of dark cotton, but it too, remarkably smelled clean.

She smirked to herself; she'd seen bears at pretty close hand before. Could he be more frightening then being under the control of these Gypsies? But Margarite, knew at this moment she hadn't the strength to run or fight. She had to find out where she was, figure out what to do. Surely her papa, her family, the sheriff, they would come after her, find her.

Lisa was leaning against a tree carefully tearing the wings from a butterfly. When Margarite stepped out to her she threw the remains on the ground, speaking matter-of-factly, you can continue to fight and resist or I can put the rope tie on again and tie you when we return. Margarite shook her head "Why bother," she said, "I don't know where I am." "Yes," replied Lisa, "You don't. You can sleep with me in our tent tonight. Come, I'll show you."

As they passed the pasture fence, Margarite walked closer, "Is that you Show?" she whispered. He came to her, "Oh," she exclaimed. "You have our Show. Sam will come for him. It's his favorite horse."

"He is a pretty one," and Lisa put out her hand and patted him as Margarite was doing. "Sam will have to find him first," she said. "And even if he does he won't be able to come on our land. Unless of course he might want to buy him back." "Buy him back," said Margarite, "You Gypsies stole him. It's against the law," shouted Margarite! "Against whose law," smiled Lisa?

"Against decent people's laws, against God's laws," came back Margarite.

Lisa turned an walked away. "You'll see," she said, "Your Louis' daughter, they'll make you a Gypsy, return you to us." "Never" spoke Margarite. "Who is this Louis? He's supposed to be my father? Is he that Gypsy man the Durante woman claims some of the men in the town buried alive because he was chasing their daughters?" "He could have been? Is that how your people tell it?" "How else could it be? The Durante woman, my pa says doesn't know what she's talking about. No one in our town would have ever buried anyone alive. We wouldn't do such a thing."

"Oh, yes, I forgot your people are so much better than we—better than human, are you?" "Chasing after females, isn't civilized," said Margarite. "This Louis was no good or he wouldn't have been chasing after all the girls in town." Lisa laughed again, "True, your father was a bad boy—just like some of yours." "He's not my father. He couldn't be my father." "Yvonne, your grandmother, says so. She's hardly ever wrong. She says you have his eyes, his mouth, his skin, his hands. The Star of Jupiter is on your index mount—that's proof to Yvonne. You wait and see, Yvonne will have you believing it yourself. Yvonne is a great convincer, persuader—you'll see," "Nonsense," and Margarite shook her head with a fury.

Chapter 11

Pa waited wearily, it was half past six—no call as yet. Paul kept saying it would take them awhile to get there. Seth's only been there once before, no telling what they could see or find out this late in the day. Linney called and told Frank to come, they were waiting for him for supper, might just as well wait at home as there. Paul said, "She's right Frank, go home, you know I'll call you as soon as there is word."

Frank went home. Supper was unusually quite, solemn for their family. You could say it was almost as though there had been a death in the family. Everyone but Johnny, feeling responsible some how, blaming themselves!

Supper over, Grandma kept Johnny, Dori busy playing Domino's. Linney busied herself with first one little chore after the other in the kitchen; and Pa sat sipping his third cup of coffee, trying to think what could possibly be done.

The call came about a quarter to nine. Walt and Seth were back at the Ranger Station. They had found the old farmhouse and the Gypsy camp, but no sight of Margarite. Seth had gotten the attention of two grade school age boys. They gave them some beef jerky in return for telling them if anyone new had come into camp when the wagons returned. Oh yes, there was a girl. A tall girl with a bow in her hair. "Was she wearing a gray dress?" "Yes!"

And the other volunteered, "She was mad, so they tied her to a tree in the back with the little kids."

"Sounds most likely that it's true. Margarite is there as we thought. I wouldn't tell the family about tying her to a tree. It won't help them and will make little difference at this point." "Precisely, what I was thinking. I won't!" "Talk to you tomorrow, after I see that Durante woman."

"Yes, of course," said Frank.

Pa explained to everyone what and how they had gotten the information. Grandma said, "Thank the Lord she's well and she's all right." Dori said, "Margarite is coming back to us, isn't she Papa?" "Yes Dori, of course she is." Linney put her arm around Dori and beckoned to Johnny, "Time for bed. Tomorrow may be a long day".

Leaving the kitchen, Pa looked at Grandma, straight into her eyes, "Margarite, you don't' know of any reason whatever that the Gypsies would take your namesake in particular or want she and Dori?" Grandma looked at him strangely, "Why do you ask me that Frank?" "Because," said Frank. I was asked that same question twice today and one questioner was so kind as to insinuate that Margarite might not be my child." "Frank," said Grandma, "We're not going back over all those outlandish rumors about the gypsy fellow and his paramours, surely you don't think anything so outrageous concerning Linney?" "I know she was in a state when I first met her," said Frank. "Well and what else, her intended leaving, just taking off!" "Yes of course," said Frank. "But you knew more about the goings on of that gypsy fellow. You heard all the talk. Did anyone connect Linney directly in anyway with all those goings on?" "Frank, for heavens sake, at that time there were those who might have connected any of our young girls with that good for nothing. What would that prove? Linney would have been only twelve or thirteen at the time." "I'm sorry Margarite, but I had to ask. All that took place before my arrival, you remember." "Frank—don't start thinking that way because of people pulling things out of the past that have nothing to do with actual events." "Trouble is Margarite, who does know what the actual events were, do you?" Margarite's eyes darkened and narrowed, her whole body stiffened and she sat up straighter! "I know there was a group of men who went out to do something about him—make him leave town and never come back. This incident if it is the one the Durante woman says she saw, would have taken place about three, four, no, five years before you settled in here and took over your Uncle's lumber business. It was 1900." "Do you think they actually did bury him?" "No, I think they put him on a freight after roughing him up a bit!"

"Thank you," sighed Frank, "As always you have your wits about you and your memories strong. What you've said makes sense." "I believe it does, Frank. Don't worry," said Grandma, "There'll be a way to get our Margarite back. I think sleep is what we all need most now."

Paul, the Sheriff, called the town council together at the back of May's store a little after twelve to tell them what had transpired with the Durante lady.

Paul said, "I'm going to make this brief and to the point. We invited her and the Mayor downtown to the Police Station, ten o'clock this s'morning with a little heavy-handed politicking."

We explained to her we thought she was in cahoots with her Gypsy cousins in this matter and after a kidnapping and what we considered a major organized theft operation of our county areas and the downtown businesses that we would take steps to imprison her if she did not stop her digging operation. I explained that the two major areas she had specified had been dug up—no Body found. And furthermore if the town had taken action against her disreputable cousin it would have been in the form of a beating and tossing him in an open boxcar on a freight with the threat of never returning. Plus there had been other reports after the reported buried alive story of his being seen in town on a number of occasions for brief lengths of time—alone and with Gypsy compatriots.

She was hysterical for a few minutes, denying she had any connection with her Gypsy relatives.

Jolly, our second in-command at the Police Department,

confirmed the fact that we had complied with the demands and dug up the two areas. Even the Mayor put his statement of agreement on our conclusion and was notifying the Governor that there was nothing more to be done. Jolly added that few of the townspeople were in sympathy with her operation remembering the bad reputation of her Uncle and the meanness of the present kidnapping of one of our very own.

Mrs. Durante scoffed at this, proclaiming someone in the town new more about her uncle's death and they were hiding it.

At this point, Paul told us he and Jolly firmly, but actually walked her to the door, where a policeman was to make sure she went to the relatives of old Mr. and Mrs. Hellman, packed her things to leave on the afternoon train back to her home ground.

As Paul said—end of the Durante woman!

Chapter 12

Meanwhile, Margarite received a taste of a very different culture and not at kindly hands. If it hadn't been for little Remos sticking up for her and acting as a go-be-tween, she may not have had the courage to survive her ordeal.

Margarite woke to a strong draft of cold air from the open entrance to the tent. She stared up at the triangle sides, this wasn't one of their clothesline tents, this was a real tent. She was sleeping outside in a tent. Glad she was, she had a real mattress under her. She felt more as though she had been unconscious for a long while, not relaxed, refreshed after a good nights sleep.

How hard it had been to go to sleep. She hadn't wanted to close her eyes. She was half afraid too. But eventually exhaustion had taken control and she had fallen asleep.

All night she had been fighting, running this way and that, trying to get away, trying to find her way back home.

Lisa threw her clothes at her. "Hurry," she said—"We eat breakfast at the main house and get our work plan for the day." "Work plan," said Margarite? "Work plan," answered Lisa. "All of us gypsies work. We all have to earn our keep. Nobody plays, lies around, but the infants, everyone else does his share, pulls his weight."

On the walk up to the farm house Lisa said, "Be smart, Margarite, don't fight Yvonne, you can't win! If you do you'll find yourself locked in the woodshed out back behind the barn. Everyone will forget you. Yvonne will come to you when she feels like it, if and when she does."

"Who is she anyway," demanded Margarite. "Don't you people have laws, rules?" "We have laws, we have rules. They aren't your laws, your rules. Yvonne is in charge of all of us. When her husband was killed, she took his place. The boss job goes to the strongest, oldest most capable member—the one in the front and believe me Yvonne is a strong able leader—you'll see."

"Why does she think I'm her son's child? It's not possible." "To you, not to her. She knows what you don't know. We Gypsies have ways of finding out what's happening all over. Yvonne knew your mother in the past. She knew of your grandmother."

"Your Mother was Louis's special affection—the reality of the Star of Jupiter on his index mount."

"His special affection, what are you talking about? You people speak in riddles. How could Yvonne ever, at anytime, have known my Mother? That's crazy! That's not possible!"

Margarite turned to Lisa, the anger boiling up within her. "You people put that Gypsy woman, Mrs. Durante, to worrying the townspeople, didn't you?"

"Mrs. Durante, such a foolish, stupid little woman. She was so easy to needle, to convince, to prod. Yes, we wanted her to stir up trouble. Yes, Yvonne put her up to it. She may have seen something, but she cared nothing for Louis, the Uncle, she claims she's so concerned about. She had no special attachment to him. She is only trying to make things right, because Yvonne has made her feel guilty for not reporting what she saw that night when she was a little girl."

"Yvonne is the one who wants to know what happened to her son, how he disappeared, why he never came back after his last visit to his 'special affection.'"

"You mean—he visited my Mother, why?"

It was Lisa's turn to turn and confront Margarite. "What kind of people are you? Has your mother never told you what happened when she was a girl your age? Was it such a small thing, because we're only Gypsies? Was she embarrassed afterwards because we are no account to your people?"

"I don't know what you're talking about," answered Margarite.

They were walking up the back steps to the kitchen. Lisa, shrugged, pulled open the screen door and deliberately let it slam in Margarite's face. A slap or a kick wouldn't have been as forceful or as demeaning in come-back.

Margarite hesitated standing still at the door. Had she had a few more moments in quandary, she might have bolted for the woods but Remos opened the screen, took her hand and pulled her to the large kitchen table. No cloth, but good smelling food. Someone put a plate with eggs, ham strips and toast buttered on both sides, and a large cup of coffee at her elbow. Lisa was eating at the other end talking to two other girls. Remos set down close to her munching on toast and drinking coffee. "Aren't you too young for coffee," said Margarite. "Not here!" "Aren't you too young at home?" Margarite had to smile. It was true. She started eating. It tasted very good. The coffee was strong. She loved the taste. "Where is Yvonne?" she asked. "Don't worry," said Remos, "She won't be gone long."

"Yvonne will give you a job," said Remos, smiling. "I had chores at home," said Margarite.

"Yvonne will give you different jobs until she finds out which one you do best." "What I do best?," repeated Margarite. And she said defiantly, sarcastically, "I read best."

"That is very good" came the voice behind her. "We will have you read for a while this s'morning to the short people and play games with them out doors in the sunshine." "There isn't much sunshine now," said Margarite. "There will be," said Yvonne.

"Remos, show Margarite where the short people meet after breakfast." And so he did. He led her into the long pantry opening off on one side of the back door. There were about ten or eleven, three to five year olds all doing their own thing. Some playing with the toys, some crawling about, some running around the room screaming. "Luck" said Remos. He waved and walked away.

What was she supposed to do? She saw two or three books laying on the counter. She found a short stool and sat down as close to the middle as she could. She sat down and started to read—aloud, loud! One or two came and sat down. The one little girl started running her hand up—and down Margarite's leg. She took her hand away. The little girl put her hand back. She decided to get up and tried to get all of the children to join hands and make a circle around her stool.

Yvonne appeared at the door with another young girl, who took the hands of a child on both sides and started singing and gathering children on each side as they clamored to attach themselves singing as they went.

"What did she do," asked Margarite? "I'm not sure, but the children respond. They do what she wants them to do."

"Let's try the older group outside," said Yvonne. "They don't need help," said Margarite. "Some days they do," smiled Yvonne. Margarite was right, at least for today. They were happy, busy in their different game or play.

Yvonne said to Remos, "Take Margarite down to visit the horses."

Chapter 13

Serge went before Margarite for lunch at the house. "So!" questioned Yvonne, "How is Louis' daughter with the horses?" "No smart remarks, no fighting the situation. She has done trainer work before. Knows a little about grooming, likes to feed them, isn't afraid of any of them like some. And, Yvonne, she knows the two new ones, the gray and that brown-beauty. He wasn't eating much. He eats for her, he nuzzled her, likes her. She didn't even mind cleaning up in the barn. The only thing she yelled about was the dirty overalls I gave her to put on."

"Well, very good. Sounding more and more like Louis, likes horses, thinks she's better than everyone else, and spits out what she thinks."

Serge laughed. "Here she comes now. We'll just see what talent she has in the kitchen."

"Your lucky, Margarite, Serge tells me you did well with the horses. Some of our new ones know you. We might even be able to find some clean overalls for you by the end of the week," "Why don't you have clean overalls all the time," said Margarite? "We don't believe in washing things all the time that are used for the dirtiest jobs. They get dirty too fast." "The clothes hanging in the Caravan Cart, are they used for dirty jobs as well?" "No," laughed Yvonne, "A, but if we washed them, they wouldn't last for long. There only used for short periods of time and worn over—other clothing for play-acting." And Yvonne laughed heavily again, "Besides the dirt holds them together." "That's disgusting," said Margarite. Margarite was going to follow the others to the table. But Yvonne grabbed her by the arm and pulled her back. "Kitchen duty for the in between ages first before they sit down to food. Ettie will tell you what to do." Margarite was ready to come back, but looking into Yvonne's eyes, especially this close at hand, she decided to play it safe.

Ettie found her and set her to work with trays of food for the table. They were heavy.

Remos thanked her when she sat his plate down for him. He had such a crazy little face. His face alone almost made her laugh.

After two tray loads, she was released to sit down and wait for her plate. It was a hot, spicy tomato and macaroni mix, but it tasted very good. Canned fruit and small funny looking hard rolls. She had to admit all of the Gypsy food tasted good.

Her group washed down the tables and dried them off. Gazing out the windows past the porch looking out and up to the trees she had a strong yearning to run up the incline and walk into the woods.

She wanted to think about what Lisa had said this morning. It hadn't made sense. It didn't make any sense. How could Margarite's mother have ever known a Gypsy?

Lisa came, put her hand round her waist and pulled her back over to the tables. "Sewing time for us," she said. "Sewing time," said Margarite.

"My what a lot of material," remarked Margarite. The older lady who was setting it out on the two long tables smiled and said, "A donation from your wonderful little town." "A donation," started Margarite, and then seeing the smile she realized what the woman meant. You stole it from May's yardage store!" "So, what are you going to do about it, pick up every bolt and piece you can and run through the woods with them," smirked Lisa. "You people are terrible. Do you have any idea how much money May will lose because of this? Plus, people will not be able to buy the materials they've ordered?" "So, she can replace and lose a little money from her customers. We lose something every year and often times do not have enough to make due for the immediate necessities."

"How can you live like this," said Margarite? "Doesn't your conscience bother you?" "Conscience," said Lisa. "What's that?" Margarite just shook her head in reply.

Lisa said, "It's our job today to cut out some dresses for the little girls. We have two patterns, two different sizes, and two prints. I'll pin them on today. You watch and see how I do it. You can cut out, but you must pay strict attention to what I tell you! You can't make a mistake on this. It would mean some would go without a new dress. They all need one." "Yes, I've helped my Grandmother cut out patterns," "Good, have you done any sewing?" "Some, I can baste and hem. I know how to do some embroidery stitches and darn." "Do you!" "Have you used a sewing machine?" Margarite said, "Only for quilt squares or mending something old." "Well," Lisa said, "You do have a few talents. Yvonne will be glad to hear this." "I don't care what Yvonne will be glad to hear. Who is she to me," and she started to throw the bolt of material nearest her across the room but Lisa grabbed her hand restraining her movement. "Careful Margarite, remember what I told you the s'morning. Yvonne is your Grandmother. That's who she is to you." "That's impossible," screamed Margarite. Lisa took hold of her arm firmly, saying, "She'll prove it to you, you'll see."

"I'll never see," returned Margarite. "Perhaps!"

After two hours of the same and basting seams, Margarite broke the silence of the room with, "Do we ever rest or play?" "You and I are too old to play. We do have an hour before dinner that we can do pretty much as we please." "What does, 'do pretty much as we please', mean?" asked Margarite. "You're learning," Lisa said, "A wise question. It means, for you, that if you choose to walk a ways from the open grounds and look at the woods close-by, you are free to do so." "Aren't you all afraid I'll run away?" asked Margarite. "No." "Why not?" "Because we know you can't." "They watch us, the young men, they make sure no one goes away too far." "It's their job to keep us all safe," said the girl named Victory.

"To think, I thought Gypsies were the freest people in the world when you're really all just prisoners." "Oh, no," said Victory, "We are free to travel, take our carts far from here, see new places, visit different parts of the land, perform our plays, our circus/carnival acts, have fun, scare all you sillies who live in little towns," and she ended giggling.

Margarite stared at her in puzzlement, nothing to throw back.

Chapter 14

Even if they say they are watching us, I'll have to see, to try. It could be a bluff. They are liars as well as thieves as Grandma has said. They had to be liars to make-up a preposterous story about her own Mother, her sensitive, nervous Mother who her Grandmother and her Father protected and watched over.

So, willfully, Margarite threw her head back and struck out, going the way they had come in. How could such a fairy-tale spot of beautiful woods and pasture be owned by such hateful, terrible people?

For a short while, Margarite forgot her predicament in the beauty of the walk in the woods. From her higher point, she circled to the left above the pasture area, she could see "Show" trotting about. What a spectacular horse he was! She walked back and up a ways, further into the woods. When she turned about again to gaze on the forest below and the homestead, she recognized how much more was open to her view here only yards higher-up. Turning first one direction and then the other, her eyes picked up the twinkle of darting, flashing light. Looked almost as if someone was sending a message. Could it be lights glancing off mirrors?

Her heart was pounding strongly now, fear, it had to be. If she walked up, a short way ahead, and straight, down through the timber, she could come out through the sparse woods and onto the old logging road. From there, who knew, perhaps God would help her escape.

Her head down pondering, Margarite stepped on a crackling branch which broke her spell. She threw her head up, staring up into the darkest meanest eyes she had ever beheld. Who was he? She didn't remember meeting or seeing this fellow before.

Margarite found her body unceremoniously thrown over his shoulder, seeing the trees only from where she had stood. What an uncomfortable way to ride down the steep incline brushing the branches, watching to keep her face and head out of the way of the lowest flung branches. At top speed, sailing into the open of the compound, she found herself being partially tossed upon the ground, bumping and rolling to a shaky stop, her side lifted slightly by the toe of a black boot.

Stunned as she was, her first impulse was to grab a branch, anything she could use as a club and assail this monster. However a hand grabbed her hair and hauled her to her feet.

Margarite numb, struck dumb had her arm painfully twisted behind her back and was half pulled, half drug to the outdoor pump where Yvonne's now familiar voice shouted out, "And what do you have here?" "Our new-comer, Louis' offspring." "She wasn't trying to run through the woods and away, was she Haze?" "She was about to sprint from the high point, back down the other side." Margarite's voice returned to her, she screamed out, "That's a lie, I was only looking, walking. Lisa said we were free to walk in the wood before dinner." "Walk in the wood, not run away," said Yvonne sternly.

"Give her a good dousing under the pump, Haze. That should bring her to her senses in time for dinner."

Haze carried out Yvonne's orders swiftly and tossed Margarite to one side. Shivering in near shock, she would have cried, sobbed if it hadn't been for her anger getting the better. She threw back her head and screamed some words which shocked her. She didn't remember knowing. At the door he turned and laughed. Picking up a chunk of wood from the woodpile by the door, he threw it at her. Falling to one side, it missed her by inches.

The children from all over the yard came running to see what all the noise was about. Looking at her miserable condition they stood and laughed.

Remos to the rescue again, brought her a towel, helped her dry her hair, found a comb, helped her comb and braid it into one long braid as finally the tears rolled down her cheeks.

Margarite, exhausted, set her bruised, battered body down beside Remos, a silent, cowed person. She barely recognized what she was eating. The coffee had never tasted so good. She sat woodenly drinking her second cup.

To say that Margarite had little to say to Lisa as she bedded down would be an over statement of the greatest magnitude. She was at the close of the day, a broken animal. Thoughts did not come to her. She cared not to know why, how or for what monstrous reason she had been treated thusly. Curiosity was dissolved in the agony of her physical aches and the futility of retaliation. She closed her eyes, and took up blessed sleep.

She must have awoke screaming, slapping back with her hands until she was silenced once more by Lisa's mother who cuffed her one final slap across the mouth, trembling, eyes wide, early dawn shut her eyes once more.

Chapter 15

Margarite refused to speak, a sort of unthinking response to what to her was the incomprehensible.

Lisa applied some salve to her lip and cuts, helped her into her clothing. Yvonne came to check her charge in the morning and told Lisa to take her back and let her sleep until noon today. She would be better then.

At noon however, Margarite remained mute. She ate mechanically. She sat and basted for the hours of sewing but would say nothing, answer no questions.

Yvonne looked her over after dinner once again. She asked Remos to sit with her, hold her hand. "Give her more coffee. She should be fine," said Yvonne. She was stubborn and needed more rest.

And so, for Margarite her second day in captivity was a kind of oblivion.

On the third day, she went with Lisa, bathed, was handed another old clean dress.

She dawned her clothing by herself and braided her hair once more into its usual two braids. Her body improved, her mind unaccepting.

She found herself ravenous at breakfast. Yvonne told them to bring her a second plate, which they did.

She went through her routine with the horses like a

sleepwalker until "Show" nuzzled her. She put her head into his neck and sobbed all alone a long while, after she wiped her eyes dry with the bottom of her dress, she kissed him. He trotted back and forth to her until life sprang back into her mind and her whole body.

She felt the strength growing in her. She was an older Margarite. Her thoughts would be there, sharper than before, but her lips would be sealed. Speak she would from now on only when it advanced her particular situation. She was going home. She didn't know how, but for sure, she was going. Come hell or high water, as Grandma said.

The days passed quickly, Margarite did her chores, spoke little, but listened a lot.

Yvonne decided she had accepted her situation. She would grow to like her new home. She was young.

Margarite stopped hoping to be rescued. She couldn't escape. She was resigned.

Later when she heard Yvonne and the others talking about two men who looked like the Law hovering around as close to camp as they could get without bumping into the gypsy guards, hope revived. Apparently they had discovered the guards didn't go on duty until afternoon each day and did not stay out in the woods all night.

Two of the younger boys had been given beef jerky in the wooded area and asked questions by two unknown men on the Sunday they arrived.

She learned the Gypsies were on-guard near the house and made their rounds about the tent area at night. Not the same guards. The night fellows were older. Only four at night she heard Haze say to Yvonne. She heard one of them tell Yvonne that the Law from Stevensville would try to rescue Margarite in the daytime. He said they wouldn't try their luck in terrain little known to them at night unless they thought it was the only way. That was their way.

Saturday afternoon, the end of the first week when the

Canadian Mounty and his two back-ups rode in and asked if they could set-up a meeting with Yvonne and her officials, Margarite realized she really was in Canada. Yvonne's answer was an emphatic No. She wouldn't let them on her property. She didn't trust them. Margarite scoffed in her mind—She didn't trust them! It was their property. The Gypsies would not let them in. The Mounties pointed out that they would be going against the authority of the law of the land in which they were living.

When she heard this—she granted a fifteen-minute interview up at the timberline. They finally all agreed to this. It was set for late Sunday afternoon. A week from her arrival, it would be.

Yvonne, Haze, and two of the older night guards were to meet the Mounties and two Policemen from Stevensville.

Margarite woke late, to a commotion outside their tent. It must have been after twelve o'clock. It was close to her head. Lisa didn't wake. Margarite threw her dark print dress over her old nightgown and nearly crawled outside to see what was going on. It must have been Thursday, no Friday night. She heard the one man say, it wasn't one of their dogs. They must have killed it with a knife, from what they said. She lay flat with her ear to the edge of the tent. She crawled back into bed shivering, wondering if one or two of her own were out there in the wood, without their tracking dog.

The next morning, going to breakfast she heard Yvonne scream at the one guard that he was an idiot, why hadn't he hunted down those with the dog and let Len take care of the animal. He said they were afraid to leave their side of the tents unguarded. "If it happens again," said Yvonne, "Go for the intruder and let the Gypsies in the tents take care of their own, you fool."

It did not quite lift her hopes, yet it kept the possibility alive that they were trying. They hadn't given her up.

Margarite's hearing was becoming most acute. She observed, she noted everything, everyone. Each one of her senses had renewed itself. All of her nerve endings were taught, eager to spring into action at the least change or altercation. She was watching herself. She was most deliberate in all her movements.

Chapter 16

At home they were in a kind of holding pattern of unbelief. In the beginning Pa had thought the Sheriff and a couple of his men could have simply gone up and forcibly taken Margarite out of the Gypsy camp. It wasn't that simple. To do this would have meant taking the law into their own hands—together with breaking Canadian laws.

So, instead Sheriff Paul and the town police force were working with the Canadian Mounties to negotiate Margarite's release.

Pa was not only upset, worried and frustrated, he was downright angry answering questions as to Margarite's true identity. And since the Gypsies had stolen off with Margarite, he thought they should be able to do much more than they were doing. Paul kept explaining the whole picture had changed because of the Gypsies being given the land in Canada. They were not just a fugitive group camping on territorial lands in Canada—They owned their grounds.

Paul was getting tired and angry explaining to the storeowners and horse breeders that he could not simply ride up into Canada, take their property and return. Now the way things were, they had to file claims with the Canadian Government. It would be up to Canada to press charges and manage some kind of restitution.

The owners and townspeople were all complaining that it should not be in favor of the stealing, vagabond Gypsies?

Sunday, after church, the Cutter's were huddled at the kitchen table awaiting word from Paul or his chief deputy after the meeting they had arranged with the in charge Gypsies. Father had told them a woman, named Yvonne was in charge, Linney had given a little gasp at learning this. Grandma's eyes narrowed and her back straightened to the point of rigidity in her chair.

They had prayed together and were all hoping for the best.

The news came to them ahead of Margarite's hearing, though she was right there on the property.

Pa couldn't believe his ears, he asked Paul to repeat what he had said.

He was so shocked himself, how could he explain it, tell Linney and Grandma. And it would break Dori's heart. Johnny simply wouldn't understand.

Frank sat the phone down, and sat back down heavily in his chair. He had never exercised a prevaricating nature, but this instance must call for close to a lie.

Pa, began by saying, "This turns out to be merely a preliminary confrontation. In other words, nothing has been settled."

The Canadian Mounty took a hard line with the Yvonne woman and Paul said this made matters worse. She would not accept any legal documents proving ownership in the case of stolen goods. In Margarite's case, she claimed it was not a kidnapping , but a reclaiming of a family member. Grandma was shaking her head violently. Linney was very pale.

When the Canadian Mounty asked Yvonne, if the child was taken by force, she replied certainly not. "She was fascinated by the fortune telling and wanted to come and join us for a visit."

Paul said, they all knew this was an out and out lie, but there was no real proof, excepting Dori's story.

"Frank," asked Grandma, "How will they manage to get our little girl back?" "Frank said, "They don't know at this point." He didn't have the heart to tell her the whole truth. Yvonne had told them there was no legal way they could take Margarite back. She would not release her Granddaughter. And if they tried to kidnap her, they would be in jeopardy with the law in Canada. She deliberately laughed at the Mounty and the others and said, "Try and get your merchandise back—you can't."

Paul said his Deputy and the Mounty could hardly restrain themselves from physically carting her off as a prisoner. The Mounty told them as they left the area, that they would find a way of getting some of them in the future for pouching and/or ongoing theft—and then they could make them pay restitution for some of what they had taken in our town. The child, Margarite, was another matter. Someone, as Paul said, he had put it, would have to come up with an idea—inventive idea!

Chapter 17

Margarite heard the news of the meeting at supper. Remos came, sat down beside her with his coffee and held her hand once more. She must admit he was a comfort. She knew he most especially paid allegiance to Yvonne, yet it was a small comfort to hold his small hand and look into the thin, strange ever-moving expressions of his face.

Most, at the table, were laughing and lauding Yvonne. Victory for the Gypsies! They were giving nothing back. Let them come and try to take it back. More sneers and laughter.

Margarite thought for all her victory, Yvonne looked a little tired, a little worn out. Would this mean they would stop trying to get her? Margarite faced her predicament. No, Father, Grandma, the Sheriff wouldn't give up. Yet when, how could they help? For a moment Margarite allowed the hate to settle in her eyes. She stared down at Yvonne at the end of the table, her head bent over her food. She continued staring as if by staring her down she might obliterate her—do her in.

Yvonne looked up and out. She was caught by the dead of Margarite's eyes. They held the stare in communion for two or three seconds until Margarite remembered there was danger in her staring and she turned her eyes away, down to her food.

Yvonne, lifted her eyes above the heads around her and idled in the blank stare of a few moments. This child, of Louis,' was biding her time. She hadn't given-up. My God, but she was like Louis—secretive, thinking, planning—only herself in mind. Win, come out ahead—they were like her. They didn't give up or in! Their own festered till they could come back, take over, be in charge. This slim little girl—a danger to all of them! It was time to find out exactly what she knew or didn't know, try and convince her of the truth, frighten her, keep her frightened, nervous, unsure. She had to put her under her thumb, otherwise she would be an explosion waiting to happen. Temple had returned from his scouting operations.

She'd have Temple, her brother, bring Margarite to her tent tonight. They would finish the séance they had begun over a week ago.

She'd put the Taro Cards in front of her. The pictures were a little grotesque, frightening to the young. Scare her with her own death first!

Margarite trembled as she sat down across from her tormentor. The same crystal ball, the cards stacked.

Margarite, upon being fetched to meet with her had determined not to be intimidated, only to ask questions to learn more of this Louis—and his supposed connection to her, to her Mother?

"You're liking it with us better are you Margarite?" "Yes, thank you for the clean overalls," said Margarite.

"Our manners are returning are they," observed Yvonne.

"We didn't finish your fortune telling session." "No" said Margarite, "Where has Temple been," asked Margarite. "Oh! You noticed." "He is our scout, we need to know what's out there, where we can go, where we can find our needs, where we can entertain." "I see," said Margarite. "Will we travel soon," asked Margarite? "We haven't determined that."

Yvonne placed six of the oversized Taro Cards in front of Margarite. "Ugly faces, ugly deformed creatures," remarked Margarite.

"No, they are not meant to be beautiful."

Yvonne went through the routine—naming the cards, telling what authority, what mysteries lay behind each one!

"Margarite pick a card, pick and hold it."

Margarite picked up the lady in black—a face to match Yvonne's.

"You're sure this is your choice?" "I am."

"Very well! She is the Queen of Death. Do you feel close to death tonight, Margarite?" "No!" "Then why did you choose this card?" She has the strongest, meanest looking face of all the others."

"You feel close to strength, to meanness tonight?" "Oh, yes!" said Margarite, "I do!"

"Do you wish to know what the Queen of Death has to say to you?"

"Yes, I would like to hear."

"Then, you shall."

"First," asked Margarite, "How do I know she is speaking through you and it is not you speaking for her, using her to frighten me?"

"Yes, you are your father's daughter. You ask the questions no one else asks."

"How do you know he is my father?" questioned Margarite.

"Because," said Yvonne. I knew your Mother was to have his child before she argued with him and ran away home."

Margarite actually moved back, she felt the answer strike her, shock, totally incapacitate her. She could never have imagined such an outrageous answer.

Yvonne grasped the moment, taking full advantage of it. She held Margarite in a hypnotic like trance! Your Mother, that lovely fair skinned girl loved my Louis, worshipped him."

Margarite screamed like one in pain, "She couldn't have!" "She did!" "Did she not tell you that she saved his life when she was a girl of your age?" Margarite shook her head. "Well, she did." "She took the earth off him with her hands, helped him gasp for air, helped him crawl out of his grave."

Margarite stared, swallowing her scream. "You see, that's how I knew, how we Gypsies knew there was not a man where they were digging in your town." Louis came home many times after that. But the last time when he went back to get your

63

Mother, he never returned. We looked for him everywhere. He never showed. I think he could not come back. This time he was buried for good—somewhere maybe in your town!"

"Mrs. Durante, the little orphan Gypsy girl saw them bury him. Those good men of your town. There was another who watched closer by, riveted, scared to death, behind a tree, she saw, heard it all. It was your Mother!"

Margarite, entranced, shook her head.

Margarite stood, and ran from the tent.

Temple started to follow, to grab her, to bring her back. Yvonne held him, "No," she commanded, "She's only upset and frightened. She will run herself out in circles on the ground. She knows not what she's about. When she, flings herself out in exhaustion on the grounds—we'll pick her up and put her in her bed with Lisa."

"Are you sure," said Temple. "Of course, look—now—she's fallen-over there, not a hundred yards away. She'll cry it out now, let her be."

Hours later, Margarite woke, lying on top of the bed, still fully clothed, a blanket tossed over her.

She couldn't determine the hour. She lay and listened to hear the footsteps of the sentries outside. When she'd heard one pass, she got up, threw the blanket across her shoulders, half walking, half hunching down, she found the pasture, the barn.

She felt herself moving to some pre-arranged plan of which her mind seemed to have no knowledge. She found "Show" in his stall. She was afraid he might whinny, but no, he just nuzzled her. She threw her blanket over his back, she threw some feed in both pockets of the old dress. She took a short length of rope, made a simple slipknot about his neck in order to lead him. She whispered to him ever so softly, "Show" "We're for it, you will know the way home, you must do it for the both of us."

As stealthfully as she could go she led him out, fastening the wooden latch of the barn, searching, scanning with her eyes where the tent sentries might be. She walked him down a way and over to the timber that fringed a part of the pasture. So far, so good. He followed her easily. Did he sense the danger? Did he understand? When they were going threw the timber up over the high point, she looked back, all was still.

Barely breathing as they stepped out onto the old logging road, she remembered they had turned off the rutted path road to the left, so, she turned "Show" to the right, walked a ways, prayed and said, "Show" "You've got to help me—she found a log—dragged it over, stepped up on it and fell over his back on her tummy, he whinnied low but accepted her weight as she grabbed his neck, turned about, set up and reached for the rope.

She whispered to him again, "Please, Show, You've got to remember how to go? You've got to do it. Go, go—Show!" She put her head down on his neck, hanging on with the rope and her other hand laying down on his neck. He started to gallop.

The tears coursed down her face as she felt his movement and knew they were off.

Chapter 18

Show moved at a good gallop as though he picked up the urgency from Margarite's body. They were covering ground at a nice steady pace. Leaning forward Margarite could see better straight ahead, to both sides and the ground area as well.

Once or twice "Show" hesitated, whinnied, smelled the air. Once he stopped, pawed the ground. Margarite was about to dismount and find out what the trouble was, when he gave a leap in the air and over a fence, they went into what seemed to be a very large pasture. It looked to Margarite like they were continuing pretty much in the same direction so she didn't try to stop. It was too hard to get back up on Show's back if she didn't have to. Sure enough on the other side of the pasture was a country road. On they sped into the night.

Margarite caught herself going to sleep. She tried to breath deeply, shook her head.

Fear seized her momentarily, looking back over her shoulder she gazed into the darkness – nothing – only the stretch of hard pounded earth and here and there the trees shrouded in darkness. The steady, thud of Show's sure feet pounding in her ears! The Gypsies hadn't missed them. They didn't know – not yet. What would they do when they found she and Show missing? Margarite gasped throwing her free hand over her mouth.

Yvonne would send out some of those mean young men,

maybe Temple too. They'd go on foot or horseback – no wagons. They would be careful especially now. They wouldn't want to call attention to themselves. They wouldn't want to admit their captive had stolen away.

About sun-up, she judged four thirty or so, she thought she heard cows. A little later, she recognized a church in the small town they skirted. She was pretty sure they had visited this place one Saturday or Sunday. They stopped to rest a bit—both, for drinks in the brook. She sat down near the bank under a large Sycamore – good cover. Maybe she could rest a moment and figure where abouts they must be in relation to home. She thought they must have crossed the border, surely – the church, the town – were in the United States.

She must have slept for a few minutes, more like fifteen or twenty. She woke to Show's nuzzling her and realized she had been sleeping.

She took some of the oats from one pocket and held them in her hand for Show. At least you can have breakfast. You deserve breakfast. You're doing all the work.

Holding onto Show's lead, she mused walking along the edge of the brook. No one in sight! If the Gypsies were tracking her, they must be far behind. Pray they haven't started yet.

Margarite found a protruding tree stump not far away. She stepped up and heaved herself up onto his back again. Off they went into the woods along another even narrower country road.

She leaned her head down again and whispered to Show, that she was depending on him to take them all the way.

She judged again it must be eight or a little after, Show stopped in a nearby pasture. She smiled, he was quite a friendly horse. He liked to commune with his own kind. While he was socializing she found two apple trees, one heavy with apples, she had two, her tummy growling back at her! She gave Show the rest of the second one. She put two more in her free pocket. This time she got on Show's back from the crotch area of one of the apple trees and threw her leg over. She was getting to be a seasoned traveler. For never before had she ridden for longer than two hours or so. This was quite a ride.

Back to it again, she tried to put her mind on what Yvonne had told her. She couldn't keep her mind focused. She was too tired to think. The only thing that was important was getting home. Nothing else mattered. If they could just get home before the Gypsies caught up with them.

When she passed the old mine, Pa had shown them one summer, she was sure they were heading in the right direction. She patted Show. They stopped for water a little further on. She gave Show some more oats. She ate another apple. The sun was playing hide and seek with the clouds today. Made it hard to tell what time it was. It must be after lunchtime. They both rested awhile in the midst of a clump of trees. She was chilly and damp from the ground, when she made herself get up. She must have slept a little longer—maybe an hour or more. Her bruises still hurt.

Not seeing Show close to her, she panicked for a moment until she looked down a ways and saw he had found a trickling spring. She went down to him threw her arms around his neck. Turning, looking about her she saw they were a little higher up than she had thought when she went to sleep. They'd been traveling along this unused trail, through the woods, all day.

More wooded as they walked, but Show insisted going this direction so she followed dumbly, leading on foot, yet being led. She found some higher logs this time and got astride quickly.

Margarite was so tired, she could hardly hold her eyes open. There was a little breeze now, colder. It was starting to get dark as they passed Jasper's Dairy farm and she knew Show was taking the country route passing by their closest town—Trenton.

She tried to fasten on the fact—they were almost home.

It wasn't long, when she felt Show give a burst of energy and move into a fine gallop. He made the area fence at the back pasture and nearly threw Margarite off over his head. She'd never jumped this high before!

He trotted up to the front pasture, whinnied loud and stomped the ground. Margarite just slid off his back and before she could speak to him, Douglas appeared out of nowhere light in hand and yelled "Show." Margarite laughed from nerves and exhaustion when Doug threw his arms around her and said, "We thought we might never see the two of you again."

"Lets get Show into the barn and you up to the house."

Sam and family greeted them on the back porch. Mary took Margarite by the hand and led her into the warm kitchen.

A few minutes more and she was settled at the table with a piece of blackberry pie and the cup of coffee, not milk she had requested.

While everyone was firing questions at her, Doug called and told Frank, "Guess who just rode into our pasture tonight?" Frank said, "Show" found his way back?" "Not just Show—someone else is sitting at our kitchen table eating a large slice of blackberry pie."

Frank, "Thank God, can it be—Margarite?" "It is." She rode Show out of that Gal' Darn miserable camp. She let him have his lead. She knew he would know the way. She even did the jump over the back fence and stayed on him. She rode him Indian style, only a blanket."

"Do we bring her home to you, or …" Before he could get it out, "Tell Sam to get that great car of his going and bring our little girl home." And Sam did!

Chapter 19

Margarite found herself, tucked in her own bed after a warm bath, her clean hair tied back with a ribbon.

Dori had come to kiss her and they had touched hands across the short space between their beds in the darkness of their own bedroom.

Pa had managed to get a few of the facts of her escape and return with Show, amidst the hugging and tears. He had gleaned that she had taken Show from the barn and walked him out of the pasture and into the woods. The woods were very dense around the compound. She had remembered which direction the wagon had turned in—going into the woods—so she simply turned the opposite direction going onto the logging trail. Getting onto Show's back had been difficult, but she had thrown herself over his back and then righted herself. Show had done the rest. Margarite said he took the back way. All her family laughed at this.

The details would have to wait till morning.

Johnny ran in early in the morning, waking both of them up. Dori admonished he wasn't supposed to wake Margarite up! She was supposed to wake Margarite up! Margarite was supposed to be able to sleep until she woke up this morning. That was Pa's orders. Johnny just waved her aside, jumped upon the end of

Margarite's bed, started firing away—unending questions. For him, a seven year old, it was the most exciting adventure he'd ever heard of and his very own sister had experienced it all.

He came to get all the news to tell everyone at school. Margarite set up and grinned at him. "How did they take you out of the Carnival, Margarite? Did they take you in one of those painted wagons they ride in?" "Yes they did," said Margarite. "They bundled me up in those colored curtains in the tent—the ones we liked, do you remember Dori?" "Oh the curtains," said Dori. "And Temple, the old Gypsy, threw me over his shoulder like I was a sack of potatoes, they tied my hands and feet together and they put a gag in my mouth. I finally fell asleep; they made camp in the early morning. They did feed me! The only good thing about the Gypsies was their food. It tasted good and they gave me coffee to drink. All the rest was bad!"

Johnny couldn't ask enough questions fast enough between his Gee and Wow!! "What were the lights—that you saw when the guy grabbed you when you were trying to run away?" "I never found out for sure, Johnny, but I think they were sending signals to each other in the wood!" "Oh, ya," said Johnny, "With mirrors."

Pa stuck his head in the door and said, "Your mother's waiting breakfast, Johnny. And Dori as soon as you get your hair combed we'll see you downstairs. I've got a few questions to ask Margarite too."

Johnny went over and hugged Margarite, "You're the bravest person ever. I knew you were tough, Margarite. I just knew you'd find a way to get out of there and come home." Margarite hugged him back.

Pa wanted to know about this Yvonne person, what she was like and why a woman was in charge.

Margarite told him everything she could about Yvonne being the leader. She told him about the sentries and how everyone worked. She told him all about the camp, and the way they lived. And of course the cruel treatment she had been subjected to. How Yvonne had admitted to putting the Durante woman up to her digging operation and how the Gypsies—already knew no one was buried there. She said he was rescued before he died. That the men in our town tried to bury him, but a young girl helped uncover him and he left town." "Was that Mrs. Durante?" "No, Yvonne said she was there, but she wasn't as close as the other person." "Did she say who the other person was?" Margarite looked at her father strangely for a moment as though she couldn't remember, and she said, "No, she just knew some other girl saved him." "Saved him," said Pa? Margarite said, "She told me the Durante woman, when she was a small child, really did see the men in this town bury this Gypsy fellow in the ground, cover him with earth. She said the other girl saw it too, and when the men of the town went away, this girl went and took the earth away with her hands and helped him breath." "My God," said Pa, "Is that what she said?" "Yes." "Did you believe her, Margarite?" "I think I did. I think I do? Yvonne lied about some things, but I don't think she lied about that. She said this Gypsy, his name was Louis, came back here many times." "When the Gypsys wagons all came back," asked Pa? "I don't know, she said he didn't come back, the last time he left."

And then, the question came that Margarite knew her father would ask, had to ask.

"Why did Yvonne want to take you and Dori? Why did she pick you two? Did she say why?"

Margarite stared at her father and the big tears came into her eyes. She said Louis, this Gypsy man, was my father?"

"Yes," said Pa, "That's what they told us." Pa put his arms around her and said, "That's a lie Margarite."

Did Yvonne tell you why she thought you were Louis' daughter, her son wasn't he?" "Yes he was Yvonne's son. She told Dori and I in the beginning when she read our fortune in the crystal ball, and read my palm, that I had the 'Star of Jupiter' on the mount beneath my index finger, just like my father. She said my skin, my green eyes, my mouth were his. And when she looked into the crystal ball—she told us, described our house, and our family like she knew us and had been to our house, not like she was truly a fortune teller."

"Margarite, you don't believe in fortune telling, do you?"
"No, Papa, I don't." "Good girl."

Margarite put on her robe and walked downstairs with her Pa. "Your Mom and Grandma have your favorite breakfast for you this s'morning—hotcakes." "Oh! How good," said Margarite. Sure enough—hotcakes and crisp bacon and Grandma fixed Margarite two poached eggs, the way she liked them best.

Pa was on his way to work. Grandma, Mother, and Margarite sat down at Grandma's end of the table together. Mother even said Margarite could have a cup of coffee to finish off with this morning. And she did.

Grandma and Mother asked Dr. Mathews to come and check her out the s'morning. Grandma didn't like the bruises on her body. Margarite insisted it was nothing—just the bumps she got from that awful Gypsy who had dropped her and kicked her with his boot and all the other rough and tumble.

Regardless, Dr. Mathews came and pronounced her fit and told her she needed to sleep and get some more rest, for the next couple of days. No back to school for a few days!

Margarite agreed, she was sooo sleepy when Dr. Mathews left that she closed her eyes and slept till late afternoon.

All was well!

Chapter 20

Margarite dressed in her own clothes and braided her hair carefully into two braids as she usually wore it.

She went downstairs to see if she could help with supper, set the table. Mother and Grandma welcomed her together and told her how much better she looked—rested, her old self.

Dori was in the parlor with her two friends from school. "Your Mother and I decided you should help us finish up the canning. We still have the applesauce, two batches of relish and one more jam. You'll be a big help. Your Mother thinks it would be best to go back to school at noon or the end of the day on Monday and get your assignments to catch up on. You'll be able to catch-up with most of what you've missed during the next week. How does that sound to you, Margarite?" "It sounds like a good idea." "That's good! That's settled, then!"

Mother was basting a small chicken. The good wholesome smell of roasting chicken, sweet potatoes and string beans assailed her nostrils. Grandma was mending one of Dori's dresses.

"The Gypsies sew in the kitchen. I helped cut out dresses for the little girls. Then we basted the pieces for sewing on the machine." "It wasn't all bad, then, was it Margarite?" "No, not all."

"Grandma, did Mother ever know Yvonne? Did you ever meet Yvonne?" "No, of course not," said Grandma. "Yvonne is a liar, as we all know. She even told the authorities at the meeting that she and her brother did not kidnap you. She said you wanted to go and visit with them?" "Did she say that?" "She certainly did. You can't believe anything she says. She frightened you didn't she?" "Yes, she did. She is strong and meaner than anyone I've ever met. She's homely, she looks like a witch. Her skin is like leather."

"Well, the Gypsies live outside a lot of the time. There right out in the weather!"

"Grandma," hesitated Margarite, "Why would Yvonne say that Mama loved her son, Louis, and was going to have a baby when she ran away and came back home to you? That baby would have had to have been me, wouldn't it Grandma?" It all tumbled out before she thought.

Grandma dropped her needle, she took off her glasses. "Find the needle for me will you, Margarite." Margarite obeyed automatically, feeling on the rug near her Grandmother's feet. She found it and laid it up on the table. As she laid it down, she looked into her Grandmother's eyes. What she saw was unexpected.

Anger was what she saw in her Grandmother's eyes. Margarite stood there in astonishment and wonder. "You didn't answer my questions, Grandma?" "Your questions are outrageous, Margarite! We've just agreed that horrible woman is a liar, why would you believe that?"

"Because, Yvonne said that Mama saw the men bury the man just as Mrs. Durante did, only she was closer and she took the earth away with her hands when the men left and helped him breath. Yvonne said Louis had a special affection for Mama when she was my age because she helped save his life. I don't know why, but I believe she was telling the truth when she said that."

Grandma, had herself under control when she took Margarite's hand and patted it and she said, "My dear little girl, you've gone through too much for a child. We'll talk it out later in my room tonight."

"I'm not such a child anymore, Grandma. I won't be able to go out and play with the children anymore."

Supper for everyone accepting Grandma and Margarite was wonderfully back to normal. Everyone was so glad Margarite was back with them. Mother told Pa that Dr. Mathews had given Margarite a clean bill-of-health. She just needed to take it easy and rest a little more. She'd be ready to go back to school next week.

Supper was delicious. Margarite had nearly forgotten how good cold milk tasted.

Pa told everyone the Herald Paper wanted to interview Margarite, but he had told them "No." He gave them a little of the story of how she'd gotten away and come home. "I didn't think our girl would want to be interviewed or have her picture in the paper. She'll get enough attention without the press intervening too. You didn't really want all that newspaper hoop law, did you"? "No," smiled, Margarite.

One good thing came of your terrible adventure. Sam put out an advertisement downtown in a couple of store windows, including the Police Station, and when he bumped into me at Willies, today, he said he was taking his signs down and the reward would be yours, Margarite." Johnny and Dori both tried to talk at once. "How much is the reward," asked Dori? "Five-hundred dollars!" "Wowee!" Said Johnny. Pa said, "Now you can start your own savings account for your future." "My, that's wonderful, Frank." said Mother. "How do you like that, Margarite?" asked Pa. "I'm surprised." "Well, said Pa, Sam's done the same thing in the past when missing horses or live-stock were retrieved. Too bad all the shop-owners couldn't use this same method to get their goods or money back."

Pa reminded the family he would be leaving Wednesday morning to check out the new mill equipment in Chesterville and wouldn't be home till sometime on Friday. Just two days, Frank?" confirmed Mother.

When Johnny came back in from play, he took Grandma's place across the table from Margarite. Margarite's mind wasn't on checkers. She was waiting for her Grandmother to retire. Perhaps then she might find the answers to her strange questions.

Chapter 21

Margarite got ready for bed, put on her robe, walked to her Grandmother's room, knocked on the door this time, instead of bursting in as she usually did. Grandma was in her robe as well, she had let her hair down and the one braid of white and gray fell against the rocker where she sat waiting for Margarite.

Grandma looked old tonight, not like her strong, vibrant self. Her whole form had shrunk. She might have been a rag doll who had lost it's stuffing and lay limp against the cushions of the rocker.

Margarite sat down on the footstool at her Grandma's feet.

"You know" said Grandma, "I would tell you nothing but the truth."

"Yes, Grandma."

"Your Mother was the girl that saved the Gypsie's life. She was your age. His name was Louis. He was the Uncle of the Durante woman. He was the one who chased the young girls in town. He came back to our town when your Mother was older—at fifteen, seventeen. He came to see the girls—your Mother too. Yes, she was special to him because she had saved his life. Your Mother was enamored of him at fifteen, and seventeen even more. She was frightened of him too. He wasn't like the young men in town who she met. He was wild, strange and unpredictable. And he was very charming, flattering and handsome in a foreign, dark way. Your Mother did fall in love with him. She used to wait, anticipate when he would come again."

"Your Grandfather and I sent Linney, your Mother, to stay with her Aunt in Chesterville for a while. We wanted her to meet some good young fellows and forget Louis. Your Aunt introduced her to a number of eligible young men. And she had a marriage proposal, but the young man was called back East when his father was dying and he never returned."

"Linney had forgotten Louis, she would have been alright but for this unfortunate turn in events. And then luckily your Father came to town."

Margarite looked relieved, "But Grandma, why did Yvonne say that Mama had lived with them and was going to have a baby?"

Grandma straightened and she said, "Oh, Margarite, I think Yvonne is just a bitter old woman and wants to get back at anyone connected to her Louis—who she loved better than anyone else. But she knew he would come to no good in the end. She wants to blame his death on everyone. But, himself is where it belongs."

"Grandma, Yvonne said, "Louis never came back from our town the last time he visited. She didn't say she knew he was dead. She doesn't know what happened to him. That's why she tried to stir up trouble and why she took me to her camp. I think she thought she would find out what happened to her son. She thought I knew something!"

"Did she?" said Grandma. "What a despicable woman. Louis, her son, was a thief, a vagrant. He trifled, teased the girls only for his own pleasure and amusement. He bragged and laughed about it with others. He cared nothing for anyone including his Mother, Yvonne. He was a very bad man, Margarite."

"But," Margarite insisted, he must have loved Mother better than some because she had saved his life."

"If you want to believe so," said Grandmother. "Now, Margarite, it's late and I'm very tired tonight. And remember now, this is our confidence, our understanding, just between you and I. You won't talk to your Mother. It would only upset her too much." "No, I won't." answered Margarite.

"Are these unhappy experiences? Is this why Mother is nervous and gets upset easily?" "Yes, it is dear. And Margarite there's no reason to talk to Papa about this. He knows of your Mother's engagement being broken-off before she met him." "Oh, yes, Grandma, I understand."

Margarite said goodnight and kissed her Grandma on the cheek.

Margarite slept very poorly. She kept dreaming and waking, and dreaming, and waking yet again.

Going to sleep with the questions, the answers in her mind—a jumble. First Grandma's face, then Yvonne's, then her Mother's and the Gypsy man who looked like her. What happened to him? Did her Mother hate her, why? Did Grandma tell her all of the truth?

The same dream! Margarite was running in the drizzle, in the damp of early morning, picking up speed as she went. Who was she? Running first on the squares of the sidewalk, then running in the wood. She was running for refuge. Escape, a place to hide! Fright, wasn't the word—panic—was the emotion! The panic came with a realization—a truth—all the pieces had come together to disclose one fact. It couldn't be otherwise, she had tried to think it away, but it remained. It was as if all the little bits had collided and fallen into place and stuck there now in a picture that could not be erased. It was too real and true to unthink. It refused to blow away. It was here to stay.

How could it be? Truth would not allow human kind to hide—it thrust forth for all to see. Like the stained glass window—all the different shapes and colors. They shouldn't fit, but they did!

Margarite woke: What was she going to do? What could she do?

Chapter 22

It was a beautiful autumn day. The three of there heads together, back and forth, would have shown anyone their happiness, their caring for each other. Linney sang some of her favorite songs, "After the Ball" and "I Wonder Who's Kissing Her Now," Margarite and Grandma singing along, a little too.

Margarite remarked, "Mother, you have a beautiful voice." And Grandma agreed, "Doesn't she though."

They finished canning the applesauce and had the relish cooking in preparation.

Grandma took up soup for all three, Margarite made toast and they had the remaining applesauce for dessert.

Grandma said, "I'm going to take a little nap in the rocker here in the kitchen. Why don't you catch Margarite up on her piano lessons Linney. She's going to have plenty of catch-up school work this next week to keep her busy." "Mama," said Linney, "You are right as always."

The piano stood in the front parlor making it convenient for Linney's piano students and a little less noisy for the rest of the household.

Mama went over the piece Margarite had been playing the week before the Carnival. Margarite played it through and Linney stood leaning over her daughter's shoulder reminding her as always of the weak spots and said, "We'll just do this one again for this upcoming week, no new piece." "Mama can I do a dance piece, next?" "I suppose you could." "The Gypsies did some really fast dance pieces. The one old man on a concertina." "A Hungarian dance, probably," said Mama. "Mama, have you ever been in a Gypsy camp?" "What kind of a question is that, Margarite?" "Not everything was bad in the Gypsy camp. Their music and their food was good."

Margarite, turned full around facing her Mother who was still standing. She felt so happy today. She felt like her Mother did care for her and love her. Maybe the hate was gone away.

She looked straight up into her Mother's face and said, "Mama, why did you hate me sometimes, especially when I was a little girl?"

Linney stared at her daughter incomprehensibly for a moment. "Did it seem to you as though I hated you," she implored? "Oh, you did at times, Mama. When I couldn't tie my shoes, when I was little, when I tripped and fell down on the steps, you just looked at me and laughed. And whenever I was laughing and having a good time giggling, being silly, you gave me mean looks. You slapped my face twice when I was young and Dori—was acting the same and you didn't slap her. Why did you hate me, Mama? Do you still hate me? I thought you liked me better the last couple of years when I was being the big-sister, and watching out for Dori and Johnny."

Linney fell into the comfortable chair on the other side of the room. Her face pale, her breath was coming in spurts. Her eyes became mean as if Margarite had accused her of a crime. "How dare you ask your own Mother questions like this," her voice was spasmatic."

Margarite didn't know what to say, what to do. It seemed to her as if her Mother had become someone else. She didn't know this person. And then she realized, her Mother looked ill, faint, as happened to her at times, and she was the cause. How could she have done this when the day had gone so well? She had promised Grandma.

"Oh, Mama, I'm so sorry, I didn't mean to make you ill." She went over and threw her head in her mother's lap, sobbing.

Linney half rose in her chair, upsetting Margarite and she slapped Margarite across the face. Margarite, fell backward in shock. "Get up," Linney screamed at her, "Get out of my sight, go to your room!"

Margarite stood, staring at her Mother, unmoving.

"Did you hear me," screamed Linney, "Get out of my sight!"

"I'll not go," said Margarite. "I'm not a small child anymore. I have a right as a person to ask you these questions. How could you be my Mother? Grandmother has been my Mother. She's napping in the kitchen. She's not here to take your side, to protect you. Oh, I forgot, Mother, I'm so sorry you're so delicate, so pale-skinned, so weak? Are you weak Mother? You weren't weak a moment ago when you slapped me, when you told me to go?"

"Are you the 'special affection girl' that Louis loved? Are you the one who worshipped the ground Louis walked on as Yvonne, his mother, said?" Did you take the earth away from his grave with your hands and help him breath, Mama—when you were my age? Grandma said you did."

"What's the matter Mama, aren't you strong enough to stand up for yourself, all alone? I had to!"

Linney had turned to stone! She said, "Help me walk upstairs to my room, and leave me alone."

Margarite unnerved took her Mother's arm and they walked up the stairs as silently as death. Margarite waited at the door for her Mother to lie down on her bed. "Go," said Linney. "Close the door." Margarite did, trembling and close to tears once more.

Chapter 23

Lynette closed her eyes. She was a child again. Just Margarite's age. So deserted the streets, a little before dawn! Not a sound, even the rain was silent. The dampness left nothing untouched, not even the bones. It enveloped you. You were sure you could never be dry again. You wanted to hurry to get home as fast as you could. You wanted to be caught up in the running as you were in the dampness.

She searched all the corners of the picture. The picture she had tried so hard to obliterate. But there it was with all the accompanying feelings. It was as real as it was so long ago. Nothing ever really died in the mind. Impressions once made, could never be destroyed. They remained. The stronger the emotion—the brighter and more complete the image! It's baffling that time has no place in the memory. Only intensity of emotion registers!

The memory can be more real than the events of the present day!

Voices, so distinct, especially in the near dark, when the face wasn't present. How strange, how solemn to hear the voices and not recognize them, or had she recognized them immediately, the one at least. She hadn't wanted to admit to herself! Linney couldn't ever remember having heard voices this way before without the faces to go with them. It had been like listening at the kitchen door before Christmas, but then she had known exactly who was on the other side. How could voices be strange and familiar simultaneously?

His face, there it was in her mind, just the way he had looked when he rubbed the dirt away and she recognized who he must be. Those dark brows and those magnificent smiling, watery eyes. Those eyes—they were always so startling—so unexpected. They were green, and you were expecting brown. The nose, sharp, almost gaunt. It wasn't a handsome face, and yet he was handsome. He was laughing. He was always laughing. It wasn't really laughter—it was amusement! Usually it was mockery—at everyone, anyone else, himself even, the world. Life was a prank, a joke.

She opened her eyes, and then closed them quickly again to see if the picture would remain and it did. It was sharp! He was standing, looking down at her, touching her cheek, running his finger down her bodice. He tilted her chin, looking into her eyes. There were tears there. She tried to step back. Her whole body shuddered—not form the cold this time.

He laughed and whispered, the same word, over and over close to her face, and finally, it must have been because of the mixture of tears and fear in her eyes which made him repeat in English, 'My Savior'! A woman, a girl, to be a woman and he laughed and ran his finger down the front of her dress. He took her firmly by the shoulders and said, "I'll never forget you."

Linney opened her eyes and found herself shivering as she had so long ago.

She stood twisting her hands in and out, as though by so doing she could make what had happened go away, disappear.

Why had she decided to go home early, not stay to breakfast in the morning as her girl-friend had expected her to do? If she had only gone back to sleep; it would never have happened. He might have died then, buried there. She half smiled—he wouldn't have stayed buried—not him. Someone else would have come to his rescue. Some other woman, some other girl would have found him. Or he would have found a way alone. She shuddered again, and sat up on the edge of the bed.

It was true, in life, that one small chance happening could

change all the rest of your life. No, not merely change—distort, irrevocably tear apart!

How little she knew that person who tore her life asunder. She was never even sure when he arrived in town and when he left. It had taken from her thirteenth to her eighteenth birthday to begin to fathom his evasions. The final discovery of what he was, was an agony, a treachery that gradually over the long years had hardened into indifference.

Back, back to the thirteen year old she was. Back to the beginning of realization and with its coming, childhood lost forever, crushed out. Back to the wondrous, careless freedom! Back to the slavery and bondage of the awful truth. Back to that first grown-up state of which she had so long envied, yearned for. Back to the thrill of discovery when the pieces fit together and gave out one answer. Back to the fright and constant vigilance. Back to the trembling, self-conscious state of alternating truth and doubt, that transfixed and fluctuated without advance or change—held in a frame—unable to acquire, blame, repress, or quite regret. Up to date, she was. Not quite live, but not dead!

Her body would not allow more, she went to sleep, which seemed like years passing, but in actuality was not quite twenty minutes.

In her dream, Yvonne was slapping her, calling her names. She was crawling on the floor to escape her boots and the brutal kicking. She'd kill her baby, if she didn't get away. Yvonne's so jealous!

Waking, her mind in turmoil. Why, how could she have struck Margarite? Those cruel words, might not have come, if… ,yes, she did have a right to ask you why you hated her. What had she ever done to deserve your hate? How could she know you were hating her father? How could she know she reminded you of his mocking ways when she laughed and giggled? How could she, Linney, possibly tell her, Margarite, a young girl, how she hated her even before she was born. How could she explain to anyone, to herself, her confusion of love and hate with Louis.

Margarite has grown into such a good, strong, young person. You've got to let her know you like and respect her. Love is not yours to give. I can't love her, but I can like her. She must have been so unhappy, so many times as a child and I paid little or no attention. I—to busy preserving my, "good mother," image—pushing the past away!

Chapter 24

Nearly four o'clock when Linney came into the kitchen. Grandma and Margarite were placing the relish jars in two rows. They were all but sealed.

"See, what you missed dear," said Grandma. "We can do the apple butter and the apricot jam tomorrow." "That's lovely, Mother."

"You feeling better after your rest!" "Yes, very much better."

Linney looked at her daughter carefully, to see if her countenance reflected calm. It did. She half smiled at Margarite. Margarite said, "Mother, I might be a cook yet. Grandma showed me how to make dressing for the veal wraps." Linney put her arm around her daughter's waist and smiled, "I have a feeling with your Grandmother's help you will." They all smiled.

Dinner went well, unusual without Papa. Dori, Margarite and Johnny talked more than normal.

Grandma promised caramel popcorn balls for later in the evening. Dori finished her homework early so as to join in a game or two.

Falling into bed, Margarite mused, the Gypsy camp faded into vagueness. Had it been real? Did it happen? Oh yes, it had been too, too real. Lisa's, Yvonne's words about her Mother. She closed her eyes and Remos came and held her hand, comforted her. What a strange little face he had. Could Louis really have been her father? What had happened to him. Did he leave Stevensville? Did someone bury him a second time? This time was he dead when they buried him? Yvonne said, he never came back the last time. Did he come here to Grandma's house? It was Grandma's house before Pa bought it. Margarite smiled, so easy for Grandma, she moved from the front to the back bedroom. Margarite liked the back bedroom best. It was a little bigger really and who wanted to look out at the houses across the street, when instead you could look out on the long stretch of the backyard with the fruit trees and the barn at the very end of the back property. No horse anymore! And she saw Show and heard Sam saying, "You can come and visit him anytime." Sam and Doug laughing! Doug saying, "We'll put a good saddle on him for you this time."

The warmth of those wonderful happenings closed around her and carried her off to sleep.

Margarite awoke with a start. She felt a strange breeze across her face. She looked across Dori's bed to the window to see if it was closed. It was. She sat up for a moment and her left hand felt numb on one side as though she had been sleeping on it. Nothing new, she'd crushed her fingers in sleep before. And then she thought of the 'Star of Jupiter' on the mount beneath her index finger. She put on her robe and tiptoed out of the room so as not to wake her sister. She walked down quietly to the kitchen. She wasn't sure why. She turned on the small light near the backdoor. When she put her hand up to peer out the window of the back door, and pulled it back, she gasped beholding the white mark of the Gypsy cross on her mount. It had never been so clear! "Why!" said Margarite. "What am I to do?" When she looked out once more the moon was nearly full. A shiver ran down her back. She turned and looked at the large old clock on the wall. A quarter to twelve. "The witching hour," she whispered and half laughed.

As she turned back, she wondered if Pa would let her have a horse of her own and keep it in the barn. After all, they didn't use it for anything much anymore—old belongings and extra corded wood.

On impulse she decided to take a quick look and see if there would be a good space, or if there was still a stall or two—there used to be. She remembered Grandma saying she had a horse when she was a young lady, before she had married.

She lighted the old lantern in the pantry and walked down to the barn. It was cool out, but not cold—a beautiful autumn night! She lifted the wooden arm piece up an walked in. It was musty like the gypsy wagon. It was bigger than Margarite had remembered.

Overjoyed, Margarite spied the two stalls close to the barn opening on the left side. She sauntered over to check them out. There was even a strap and a bit on the harness hook in the furthest stall over. She looked all around in each. They looked ok. Funny though, the earth in the furthest one over was so uneven as though it had been dug up for some reason and never smoothed over evenly. When she pushed the old hay particles to one side it was even more uneven and strange looking than she had noticed at first. She walked back to the first stall and brushed the straw bits out of the way with her slipper and found it was harder pressed and even. Yvonne thought most barns had special treatment for the floors of the stalls.

Puzzled, she stepped back once again, staring at the unevenness of the floor. It looked like someone had been in a great hurry to put the earth back. They had been quite careless and uncaring.

Why would they have dug here? Margarite caught her breath and her own body balance, putting out her left hand, grabbing onto the old board side of the stall. "No," said Margarite, "You are thinking like a child—like a story—in a book."

Trembling she stood unnerved, alarmed at the thought that was hammering in her mind. She would have to know, to find out. No one at the house knew. They were all fast asleep.

She looked about her for the instrument she needed. It was leaning in a corner by the woodpile on the opposite side of the barn.

She carefully set the lantern down, walked over and drug the shovel behind her.

Hitting at the dirt over and over with the sharp edge of the shovel to loosen the harder shell of the top crust. In, under the very top it should be looser like it had been at the dig not too far from the railroad tracks.

Margarite lost track of time, so bent on her project was she. She was about to stop, thinking how foolish she had been and worrying how she was going to get the earth back and cover it over with odds and ends or something so it would not look as though the earth had been loosened here, when the shovel gave off a clinking sound. Had she hit rock here? She got down on her haunches, pushing back the earth in the shallow center of the dig. Pushing back a little further she saw what looked to be a tooled piece of silver. It looked like, it was—a belt buckle. Really terrified, but intensely curious she brushed back as much earth in the near vicinity of what looked like a belt buckle as she could easily push away. It wasn't but it must be—bone, a skeleton, and she clamped her hand over her mouth, and caught on one edge of the shovel blade was a dark piece of material. She held her breath. For a moment she was sure she was losing consciousness. She placed the shovel carefully against the wall of the stall.

Picking the lantern up she looked more closely at her find in the more direct light. It was a belt-buckle for sure, and it must be a part of a leg bone she had touched with the shovel. She turned, intending to find a spot to sit down when she realized she wasn't alone!

She held the lantern higher, "Grandma, oh you scared me."

"What on earth are you doing out here, Margarite?"

"Grandma, what are you doing out here? Why did you come out here?" "I came out, because I saw a light in what looked to be the barn, and since your Father is not home, I came out to see, myself who was wandering around on our premises. And I find you. What are you doing?"

"I woke, I couldn't go back to sleep. And before I went to sleep I was thinking about Show and wondering if Pa would let me have a horse of my own. So I just decided to come and see if we still had stalls. And we do."

"Of course we have stalls," said Grandma. And she walked over closer to Margarite.

Grandma stared down at the ground, "My God, Margarite, what have you done?"

Chapter 25

Margarite struggled to find words to explain to Grandma what she had done and why.

They stood there both staring down now at the open ground and the light bouncing off the silver at the near center.

The barn door creaked and they turned to see Linney stepping into the barn carrying a lantern like Margarite's. "Oh my God," whispered Grandma! "Not Linney. She can't see this. What are we going to do?"

Grandma turned, "Linney this foolish girl of ours came out to see if we had stalls for horses in the barn. She couldn't sleep, so she came out to see." Pushing Margarite out in front of her as she spoke, Grandma moved away from the scene picking up Margarite's lantern.

"Oh my goodness, of all things. I saw the light when I woke. That dog of Christopher's woke me again. My, said Linney, You both look as if you've seen a ghost or share a guilty secret."

Linney held her lantern and moved passed them on the right, well of course, there are still the two stalls for horses. "What is this, who's been digging?" screamed Linney. "Oh, no, no," screamed Linney. She got down on the ground and touched the silver buckle. "No," she screamed again. "Ma, you told me it didn't' happen, my dream. It was just a bad dream. He wasn't dead, he ran away. He didn't run away. He is dead! Oh, no Louis,

I didn't mean it. I don't want you to die. You should die for what you're trying to do to me! You've ruined my life and you don't care. You don't love me as I love you, you never have. You don't care for anyone but yourself."

Linney hysterically dug in the earth uncovering more of the skeleton.

Margarite stood, dumb, transfixed, unable to move.

When life flowed back into her veins she found Grandma fallen against the stall wall. It must have supported as she fell against it.

Margarite stood not knowing what to do, where to turn.

She went to her Grandmother. She tried to lift her up, but couldn't. She slapped her hands. "Unconscious, she's passed out, what will I do?" Her Mother crazed. Margarite, shook her by the shoulders and half pulled to get her to her feet. She looked at her staring eyes. And she slapped her across the face repeatedly until expression came back into her eyes. Mama, you've got to help me get Grandma into the house. She's unconscious. Please, Mama help me." Margarite set the one lantern on top of the stall wall and picking the other one up. She pulled her mother over to her Grandmother and mechanically she followed Margarite's instructions. You get her under her other arm and we'll take her back to the house. With the lantern in one hand and Grandma hoisted under her other arm they half pulled, half dragged Grandma to the house.

Margarite said, "Mama, open the door, I'll drag Grandma under her arms to the door." They laid Grandma down on the sofa in the family parlor. Margarite said, "Mama put her head-up on the pillow—here and hold her hand, I'll call Dr. Mathews."

When he got there Margarite had washed her Mother's hands and had helped her change into another robe. She sat holding Grandma's hand while Dr. Mathews brought his patient to and told them quietly, she's had a little stroke. I don't think it will have done a great deal of damage, I'm going to give her something so she will sleep for a while. Let's get some more pillows. You take off her outer garment and get some blankets and make her comfortable right here.

Grandma came to and struggled to say a few words to the doctor. And when she saw she was in the house and we were alright, she sighed and in a few more minutes closed her eyes. Dr. Mathews told us she would sleep for quite a while, probably—one of us should stay here with her.

Linney said, "Of course, I will. Margarite made coffee for her mother. And then she kissed her on the cheek. She said, "Mama you'll be alright now won't you? I'm going to straighten up in the barn."

Linney said, "Yes, someone will have to."

Margarite looked at the clock—three-thirty, everything should be straight when Dori and Johnny come down for breakfast. They could warm Grandma's cinnamon rolls that would be easy and fast."

She turned her lantern—out and put it away.

The barn was as they had left it. She picked up the shovel, but before she started throwing the mounds of earth back in place, she carefully pulled, and gratefully the buckle gave. She found herself holding it in the palm of her left hand. It was a strange, though warm feeling. Margarite had the eerie feeling of setting the past right. Of making amends. Of closing a book. She sat the buckle out away from the dig. As quickly and efficiently as she could she covered the shallow grave, the tears cascading down her cheeks dropping into the soft loose unsubstantial earth. After smoothing as well as she could, she found the large loose gravel in the same corner where the shovel had stood. It must be what Papa had left when he had put in the walk area between the two gardens last summer.

She prayed as she threw them out that they would cover all of the torn up area. They did a little better than she had hoped. She emptied the bag on top of the first stall so they looked much the same.

She remembered that before putting in more soil, horseman did this to make the new topsoil more substantial. And she would ask if she could not use some of her reward money for this and the horse she wanted so much.

Margarite lifted the buckle in her hand once more. She

carefully put it in her pocket, took her lantern, and latched the barn.

The sun was coming up. She looked about her for a moment. Then with swift, deliberate stride, Margarite walked down to the big old oak at the divide of the property walking carefully around it until she found the spot she remembered playing under when she felt sad or alone. She got down on her knees and found the place where she had wedged her baby ring Grandma had given her for a keepsake. She smiled. It was there, more covered with earth and moss bits, the hanky—but her ring was inside. She put the buckle and ring together, rewrapping and stuffed them even further down and into the root of the old tree—pulling the loose, earth over the hanky. Pulling her hand out, she let the loose soil flow through her fingers.